P9-CJH-094

Queen Cindy Ratzlaff

Queen Kathy Kinney

QUEEN
OF YOUR OWN
LIFE

KATHY KINNEY & CINDY RATZLAFF

QUEEN
OF YOUR OWN
LIFE

THE GROWN-UP WOMAN'S GUIDE
TO CLAIMING HAPPINESS AND GETTING THE
LIFE YOU DESERVE

HARLEQUIN®

QUEEN OF YOUR OWN LIFE®

ISBN-13: 978-0-373-89215-0

© 2010 by Kathy Kinney and Cindy Ratzlaff

All rights reserved. The reproduction, transmission or utilization of this work in whole or in part in any form by any electronic, mechanical or other means, now known or hereafter invented, including xerography, photocopying and recording, or in any information storage or retrieval system, is forbidden without the written permission of the publisher. For permission please contact Harlequin Enterprises Limited, 225 Duncan Mill Road, Don Mills, Ontario, Canada, M3B 3K9.

Library of Congress data on file with the publisher.

® and TM are trademarks owned and used by the trademark owner and/or its licensee. Trademarks indicated with ® are registered in the United States Patent and Trademark Office, the Canadian Trade Marks Office and/or other countries.

www.eHarlequin.com

Printed in U.S.A.

To every woman we have ever met or have yet to meet—thank you for your inspiration, laughter and friendship. We dedicate this book to you.

ACKNOWLEDGMENTS

First of all thank you to our amazing agent, Stephanie Tade—you shared our vision from the beginning and helped us find the perfect home for our book. Your encouragement and guidance have been a gift.

Secondly thank you, Deb Brody, our brilliant editor—your clarity and advice took us exactly where we needed to go on this journey. We couldn't have done it without you.

Also, thank you to our family and friends for your patience and love during the long months of writing, video chatting and business trips. We know it's not always easy to be part of the "royal family."

CONTENTS

INTRODUCTION

Welcome to the second half of your life, or what we believe can be the *best* half of your life!

Queen of Your Own Life is a philosophy, a decision and an invitation to happiness for women who have made the tough but rewarding journey to the midpoint in their lives. We're excited to be your guides on this next big adventure.

With humor and common sense we will offer you our tried-and-true actions to blast away at the societal tall tale that young is beautiful and old is just old. With our seven simple steps we will help you let go of the negative thoughts that keep you from fully admiring and accepting yourself just the way you are—a woman in full bloom, valuable, sensual, vibrant, wise and more beautiful than ever.

Every significant stage of life is marked by a celebration or ritual—birth, graduation, marriage, even death—yet we have nothing to mark the momentous accomplishment of reaching midlife. That is, unless you count the horrible tradition of over-the-hill birthday parties, complete with black balloons, coffin-shaped cakes and gift bags filled with incontinence supplies. Yuck. That's the "celebration" society sets up for women as we reach midlife? After you follow our easy, straightforward guidelines to claiming your crown, we'll help you plan one hell of a kick-ass Crowning Ceremony, filled with laughter and good friends, that will mark your transition into the glorious second half of your life.

If you have been feeling that the best part of your life is past, then this book will prove to you that there is always something more and that the door to being happy is not only never closed but is just waiting for you to fling it open. Remember, you don't have to be twenty to have your whole life ahead of you.

So, let's get going. It's time to become Queen of Your Own Life—if not now, when?

CHAPTER 1

crone [krō-an](noun) 1. offensive term 2. a term of abuse 3. a withered old woman 4. from Anglo-French *caroine, charoine*— dead flesh 5. a woman over forty

THE AWAKENING
· · · *or* · · ·
Why We Wrote the Book

It all started one night because Kathy's feet were hot and she couldn't sleep. While searching the Internet to see if other women had similar symptoms or if what she was experiencing was fatal, she stumbled upon several sites telling her that she had reached her crone years and must embrace entering the final phase of her life. Having an understandably violent reaction to the word *crone* she looked it up in the dictionary. That night on the Internet she learned two important things:

1. Many women have hot feet and need to kick the covers off at night to cool off.

2. *Crone* meant exactly what she thought it did and she didn't want to be one.

According to *Merriam-Webster's Dictionary* the word *crone* dates back to the fourteenth century and is a Middle English term of abuse. The dictionary under the Tools menu in Microsoft

Word agrees with *Merriam-Webster's* and adds one additional definition: woman over forty.

Kathy found Web sites that claim the title *crone* hasn't always been derogatory; in pre–Christian times, old women were particularly important members of the community. Yes, we're sure they were very important members of their society but we bet they didn't like being called a crone any more than we do. Let's face it, words matter. The language that others and we use to describe our lives and ourselves as women affects us. No matter what kind of spin you put on it, the word *crone* still evokes an image of a withered old woman at the end of her life, and that's no reason to throw a party.

There are also Web sites that offer the advice that a woman should take time alone to make the transition to crone. Alone, so that the constant waking and the tossing of covers to accommodate night sweats can be guilt free. Alone, to deal with hot flashes and to come to terms with the chaos created by hormonal changes, as well as to deal with erratic moods that may alienate family and friends. Hang on—it's bad enough you get labeled a crone but now you're supposed to go off alone? Certainly spending time by yourself can be meaningful and enriching, but isolating yourself to protect yourself and others from your symptoms of menopause while you embrace your inner crone doesn't seem like a positive way to deal with growing older. What about staying put and surrounding yourself with a community of like-minded women who will offer you love and support?

A few weeks after Kathy's visit to the Internet we met for

our annual "girlfriend getaway." That year, to celebrate our friendship and mutual love of travel, we met in the beautiful city of Prague. As always, over dinner the first night, we began by congratulating each other for not being on any kind of medication and then launched into the fun task of catching up as we were both going through many changes in our careers and relationships. It wasn't long into the conversation that Kathy dropped the C-word—*crone*—and, not surprisingly, Cindy didn't want to be one, either. We quickly reached the conclusion that, even though we were hovering on the edges of menopause, what with all the advances in science, we were probably only at the midpoint of our lives. Being a crone for the next forty or fifty years was not an attractive option.

We wondered if there was a comparable word for describing aging men and, if there was, would they allow themselves to be called that. We couldn't think of a single word that was even close. The sight of the well-lit Prague Castle out the window of our restaurant made us think of the phrase "a man is the king of his castle." What the heck does that make us—the crone in the corner? We decided, right then, that we would become Queens—Queens of Our Own Lives—and we would celebrate this transition, not in isolation, but together with friendship, joy and, hopefully, cake.

We realized we needed a format for our celebration. We thought about the kind of events that had meaning and significance to us, and how we'd like to create a new event to celebrate entering this next stage of life. Every New Year's Eve Kathy has a big dinner with a lot of candles, good food, great friends and champagne. During the course of the meal a candle is passed around the table and everyone answers these two questions when the candle comes to them: What do you want to let go of or leave behind in the old year that no longer works for you, and what do you want to keep that is still working for you? In those two sentences, often with tears, courage and much laughter, the old year is honored and put to rest and the New Year is welcomed in. We wanted something like those New Year's Eve dinners to help us let go of things from the first half of our lives that were still holding us back and to bring forward the things that we admired about ourselves. So that's what we did. We used the two questions and we called it our Crowning Ceremony.

For the next six nights over dinner we asked each other what we wanted to let go of from the first half of our lives that was no longer working, and what we wanted to keep and take to the second half that was still working. During the day we wandered, saw the sights and marveled at gorgeous Prague. At night over wonderful meals like goose and champagne or sometimes just goulash and pilsner beer, by asking these two deceptively simple questions, we began an adventure that turned into a thorough virtual spring-cleaning of our mental closets. We happily left huge piles of useless old beliefs, about fear, beauty and needing to wear high heels, in booths and under tables in restaurants all across Prague.

During the middle of our Crowning Ceremony week we started to feel that, while we had most definitely enjoyed our youth, the best of life might really be yet to come. By letting go of things like self-doubt, fear of being judged and worry about how to look younger, we were setting ourselves free to admire who we were right now. We were overjoyed to discover that we did admire the women we had become. We were two strong women, who brought with them to the second half of life courage, wisdom and, most of all, the knowledge that they could survive anything with their dignity and humor intact.

At the end of our Crowning Ceremony week, by examining our lives and asking each other these two questions, we felt strong, powerful and positive that this second half of our lives would certainly be the best half. Cindy had left her doubt about being smart enough to compete in the business world with some swans floating in the Vltava River outside a three-star seafood restaurant and was taking great pleasure in the knowledge that she was still the courageous twenty-year-old woman who had sold her bike for two hundred dollars, taken the money and moved to New York City. Kathy, leaving behind her fear of not being worthy of love, in an underground gothic café that served beer, absinthe and goulash, was elated to reclaim the sense of humor that had helped her keep a positive outlook on life since she had told her first knock-knock joke at the age of four.

Having declared ourselves Queens of Our Own Lives, we ended our vacation and returned to our homes. We were delighted to find that we both continued to feel empowered by our Crowning Ceremony. Every woman we told about our vacation loved the idea and wanted to have a Crowning Ceremony of her own. We'd had so much fun and gained such strength, we decided that the least we could do was pass it on to our friends. So we began to host gatherings that we continued to call Crowning Ceremonies.

Our first ceremony was with our friend Nancy over coffee, scrambled eggs and bacon in Las Vegas. We bought each of us a crown-shaped rhinestone brooch and made our friend an official You Are Crowned Certificate, which we signed and gave her at the end of breakfast. In keeping with becoming Queens, we had simplified the questions to: What do you want to banish from the first half of your life, and what do you want to keep? The ceremony was fun, low-key and yet transforming for our friend, who realized she needed to banish spending time caring for others who hadn't even asked for her help, so she could be a better friend to herself. Delicious bacon and eggs with good friends and an important life-altering revelation— could there be a better breakfast experience?

The next Crowning Ceremony we hosted was in a hotel room in New York City with several old friends, over glasses of wine and a large fruit plate. We went around the room and these women, whom we had known for more than twenty years, freely shared their answers to the two questions. One friend banished the feelings of being inadequate and yet another banished the need to be perfect, and we all decided that we wanted to keep our lifesaving senses of humor. We laughed, cried, ate pieces of unripe fruit that you can find only on bad fruit plates and made already good friendships even stronger. We soaked in the warmth, comfort and peace of being in a community of trusted women who, also at the midpoint in their lives, were ready to give themselves the gift of being Queens of Their Own Lives.

Each Crowning Ceremony we hosted became larger, with friends wanting to bring friends and those friends wanting to bring friends. Soon there were more strangers than friends at the celebrations. Yet, at the end of each gathering, all the women present felt the same sense of warmth, comfort and peace that we had felt at our intimate gatherings with old friends. No matter what age or level of education, whether out in the business world or working at home in the business of caring for their families, the women at these ceremonies were amazed and surprised by the revelation that they were not alone—they all had a common longing: to be given the permission to celebrate, with joy and in a community, this transition to not a crone but a mature, valuable, beautiful, strong woman.

We're not therapists (although we did both work as secretaries at the New York County District Branch of the American Psychiatric Association). We're simply two women who in more than thirty years of friendship have developed some commonsense tools and strategies to prepare ourselves to live the second half of our lives in grace, filled with the excitement of what is yet to come and the knowledge that we are beautiful just the way we are. If you're also longing for this, then we invite you to come with us on the journey.

Here are the seven gifts you'll give yourself by reading our book:

1. Claim your beauty and feel your power

2. Clean your mental closet and find your Queen voice

3. Admire yourself for who you've become

4. Build deep, fulfilling friendships with other women

5. Establish firm boundaries that will strengthen all of your relationships

6. Discover the simple trick to finally being happy

7. Proclaim yourself Queen of Your Own Life

Join us in our simple guide to laughing, crying, healing and easily making the transition into what will be the best half of your life. Remember, you don't have to be twenty to have your whole life ahead of you.

CHAPTER 2

beautiful [byoõ-tə-fəl] (adjective) 1. having qualities that give great pleasure or satisfaction to see, hear or think about; delighting the senses or mind 2. wonderful; very pleasing or satisfying 3. excellent of its kind 4. you

CLAIM YOUR BEAUTY
AND FEEL YOUR POWER
· · · *or* · · ·
How to Banish Your Inner Crone

"Mirror, mirror on the wall, who's the fairest of them all?"

"You're short, you're fat, you're old and you're gray. It certainly isn't you, so back away."

Be honest. We have all looked in the mirror and asked some version of that question and, just like the queen in *Snow White*, have been unhappy at the imagined response from our "magic mirror."

We grew up watching Disney movies in glorious Technicolor and it seemed the heroine in their movies was always a princess who was young, pretty and naive, needing to be saved by a prince, whom she marries, and lives happily ever after. Did you happen to notice in those movies that any woman over forty—heck, who are we kidding…any woman over thirty—was either a chubby, apple-cheeked godmother, a mean old crone, a cruel stepmother, an evil queen or the dreaded combo: a cruel stepmother who happened to be an evil queen with magic powers that she could use to turn herself into a mean old crone?

We blame everything on that damn magic mirror from the *Snow White* movie. When the queen asked, "Mirror, mirror on the wall, who's the fairest one of all?" the mirror said, "Lips red as roses, hair black as ebony, skin as white as…blah, blah, blah, it's Snow White." What if the mirror had said, "My Queen, why waste your emotional energy on feeling competitive with every other woman in the world? Let's take a look at YOU. You're amazing. You're beautiful, resourceful, creative and you have a real talent for sorcery. Bravo!"

What a different story that would have been! The queen could have acknowledged and admired her talents, which would have helped her low self-esteem issues (really, why did she even care what the magic mirror thought in the first place?), and Snow White could have stayed home with her family and grown up with a positive female role model. The only ones who really would have come out on the short end of the stick would be the seven dwarfs, since they would still be living in a pigsty of a cottage and cooking their own meals.

Now, please stay calm—we're not anti-Disney and we don't want to spoil the pleasure of a good fairy tale. Honestly, nobody enjoys seeing Disney movies or going to the Magic Kingdom more than we do. Space Mountain and Rock 'n' Roller Coaster Starring Aerosmith are two particular favorites. Also, Disney has worked really hard in the past few decades to change their heroines from naive, young and pretty princesses to plucky,

······················· CROWN JEWEL ·······················

So much has been said and sung of beautiful young girls, why don't somebody wake up to the beauty of old women?

—Harriet Beecher Stowe

young and pretty regular girls. We're just saying there were very few images of older, happy, loving, beautiful women to be found in the influential movies of our youth.

Remember the olden days, long before Disney started making their magic? It was critical for the survival of your family that, when it came to marrying you off, you be young and beautiful. If you were young, there was the hope that you had a lot of good breeding years ahead of you, and if you were pretty, there was a fifty-fifty chance of your offspring not resembling the family dog. With the bargaining chip of a young, pretty daughter, a father could send her off with only some warm baked goods for a dowry and, in return, could expect quite a number of fine heifers and possibly a couple of goats from the family of the future husband. A young, pretty daughter could mean the difference between a long, hungry winter for her family or a time of feast and abundance. Thankfully, those days are long gone and, now that we have the vote, most likely will not return. Unfortunately, the idea of equating youth and beauty with our value as women is still all-pervasive in our society and the bad news is we're helping keep the myth alive.

Someone once told us that our Western culture is so beauty oriented and judgmental that if a Masai chief, a great and respected warrior among his people, came to this country, within two weeks he would be filled with self-doubt, asking everyone around him, "Does my hair look okay? Is my deodorant working? Does this loincloth make me look fat?" Media messages can take the strongest and most confident among us and eat away at our self-esteem, making us second-guess ourselves and leaving us weak with anxiety. Not fun. Not fun at all.

············· CROWN JEWEL ·············

**Life is what we make it,
always has been, always will be.**
—Grandma Moses

We know it's not a new idea that we are a visual society, and how we look in real life compared to the perfection we see in movies, on TV and in magazines can be very damaging. Even women in a gulag in the middle of Siberia know by now that airbrushing, lights and special camera lenses are responsible for the dewy youth and flawless beauty that they see on-screen and in magazines. So why do so many of us still believe that trying to look younger is the key to being beautiful?

Let's go back to that damn magic mirror. Every time the queen looked in the mirror, instead of seeing herself, the mirror showed her the face of Snow White. How annoying was that? No wonder she got so mad and acted out by turning into a crone. We face the same challenge every time we read a magazine or watch TV and films—we are bombarded with images of flawless young women. Even though we know that these images are altered and the young women are probably only twelve-year-old girls, we can't help but compare our real looks with these heightened images of beauty. The media is relentless, and we're only human, so it's no wonder we sometimes feel like crones. Hopefully we don't hire a woodsman or create a poisoned piece of fruit to take out our competition, because we'd be so busy we wouldn't have time to do anything else!

The bald-faced truth is that even if a virus sent from an evil parallel world wiped out the entire entertainment industry as we know it, there would always be women who are younger, thinner, prettier, funnier, blonder and richer. If you play the comparison game, you will always lose. It is time to stop playing the game that for most of us started when we were so young we didn't even know we were playing it.

CINDY

It was seventh grade, my first year at Lincoln Junior High. The gym teacher announced that she was forming a new club—the Modern Dance Club. The chosen girls would be performing a big show at the end of the year in front of the entire school with full lights, costumes and makeup. This was my chance to move from clumsy, awkward "President's Council on Physical Fitness" failure to graceful teenage beauty. I was giddy at the prospect.

The audition required each girl to choreograph and perform a short dance piece to the musical selection of her choice. I daydreamed for hours about being in the show. I imagined that we'd wear sexy leotards and float across the stage in synchronized perfection, bathed in soft lighting, while the audience applauded wildly in awe. Then the next day I would be popular.

I rushed home and put my parents' latest Columbia Record Club pick on the big, oak Early American–style console stereo. It was by Herb Alpert and the Tijuana Brass, and as "A Taste of Honey" blared out, I flung myself from one end of the living room to the other with wild abandon. The music seemed so exotic and "dancing" to it made me feel very sexy and pretty.

The day of the auditions the orchestra room was turned into a large dressing room with pieces of black construction paper taped over the glass doors for privacy. It was heady for me just to be there, the very act a declaration that I thought I was beautiful.

There in the room with thirty-five other girls, as we changed into our leotards, I caught a glimpse of all of us in the mirror. I was suddenly overcome with doubt. I began comparing myself to the other girls and was overwhelmed by the feeling that I bulged in all the wrong places. It happened in a flash. I had been so happy a few moments before, but with one glance in the mirror I knew I'd never be a Rockette.

To me it didn't look as if any of the other girls were as nervous as I was. They didn't seem to be comparing themselves to anyone else in the room. They appeared confident, perfect and so beautiful. No amount of living-room practice had prepared me for the tidal wave of self-doubt that washed over me. As we each waited for our turn onstage, I picked up my things and ran home so fast I probably should have considered just signing up for track.

At the end of that year I went to the big dance show and here's the revelation my twelve-year-old self had: I could have been in the show, because they let everyone that was at the audition be in the club, and none of them had been very good! The dancers were all different sizes and had only about a teaspoon of talent between them and yet the show was a huge success. Everyone went home happy that night except me.

I'd like to say that this junior-high-school revelation changed the way I thought about my body and that I grew up with healthy self-esteem and never judged myself to be unattractive again, but that's not my story. In fact, for years, I engaged in a cycle of yo-yo dieting that led me to try everything from hypnosis and "fitness" tap dancing to burdock root and high colonics. I was sure that being a certain weight would change the way I felt about myself and how everyone else perceived me.

During one particular quest for body perfection I fasted

under a doctor's supervision for nearly four months and was elated to finally reach my lifetime goal weight. In the next eight hours, based on my assumption that being at my goal weight would open the doors to the world that beautiful people lived in, I made a series of "poor choices." I accepted a date with my creepy, old, lecherous diet doctor because I didn't know how to say no; I answered an ad in *Back Stage* magazine for Models Wanted, No Experience Necessary, which eventually landed me on the covers of a series of erotic novels; and then I auditioned to be a bunny at the Playboy Club. It was a long day that had nothing to do with beauty or beautiful people.

That night I met my friends for dinner. As the humiliation of the day hit me, I burst into tears. I'd given the idea of an ideal body so much power in my life that I lost my sense of self. Between sobs (mine) and laughter (theirs) I related the events of the day and proceeded to consume an enormous quantity of food…the first solid food I'd eaten in four months. By the end of the meal I was no longer at my goal weight and had ended my fast with a vengeance. My friends still refer to this as "the day Cindy weighed one hundred and ten pounds."

Needless to say, over the next few months I gained back all the weight and some of my common sense. I stopped dating the diet doctor and didn't take the job at the Playboy Club. This was just one of the many interesting adventures I'd have in my life with weight loss and regain.

CROWN JEWEL

**You grow up the day you have
your first real laugh at yourself.**
—Ethel Barrymore

Recently I was looking through a box and found one of the many diaries I had kept over the past twenty years. Every single entry started with "Today I weigh…" In that same box I found pictures of myself from a variety of decades past. Here's the funny thing—I look at those pictures now and I see a perfectly lovely girl and an attractive young woman. If only I could have looked at myself back then and seen what is so clear to me now. Ah, twenty-twenty hindsight.

• • •

It would probably not be much fun to be young again but sometimes don't you want to reach back through the years and say to your younger self, "SNAP OUT OF IT!" Still, regrets are just a waste of time because who we were then was just us on the road to who we are now.

In our original Crowning Ceremony, when we were banishing things that no longer worked for us, we decided that this

CROWN JEWEL

The really happy person is one who can enjoy the scenery when on a detour.

—Unknown

myth that we needed to be young and thin to be beautiful just had to be the first thing to go. We had wasted too much precious time and energy over the years feeling less than beautiful. This outdated belief had kept us from what we really wanted— lightness of spirit and daily happiness. We realized that, short of buying a TV network and broadcasting our message 24/7, the change in attitude had to begin with us.

KATHY

When I was in second grade my mother bought me a pair of red velvet Mary Jane shoes with little rhinestone buckles. I thought they were the most stunning shoes in the whole world. I wore them to school every day except when it snowed, which was often in Wisconsin, and then I carried them in a paper bag and put them on when I got there.

The shoes inspired me to write, produce, direct and star in

my own version of *Cinderella*. I cast some of the girls and one boy in my class to play the other roles and had them come over to my house to rehearse. I had a strong artistic vision of how the production should go and the other kids, either impressed by my passion or intimidated by my bossiness, did exactly what I told them.

On the day of the play I was so excited. We stood in front of the class and it went off perfectly. The teacher and students loved it and we got lots of applause. My friend Debbie was a beautiful and sweet Cinderella—SCREECHHHH... That's right—I wrote it, directed it, produced it and they were my shoes, yet I cast myself as one of the ugly stepsisters. I was eight years old and I already felt I wasn't pretty enough to be Cinderella. I wasn't pretty because I was fat—at least, that's the spin I put on what the other kids were saying to me.

By the time I turned thirteen I was certain I wasn't pretty. I could tell by comparing myself to the girls on the pages of *Seventeen* magazine, the bible of young womanhood, that I wasn't pretty. I felt I was the polar opposite of pretty—I had a whole face full of freckles, I was overweight and I played the viola. It all added up to certain social doom.

I needed a plan. I began to pore over all my back issues of *Seventeen* magazine. Each of them had articles about how to make yourself beautiful with cosmetics. That was it! I would learn how to make myself beautiful. I cut out every article I could find on makeup hints—such as line your eyes only from the outer corner to midiris on top and bottom to make them look wider, or blend a lighter shade of lipstick on the middle of your lower lip to make it more pouty and sexy. I was ready to take my life into my own hands and reverse my fate.

I saved my allowance and finally got the courage to buy some makeup. I remember exactly what it was. Franco Zeffirelli's movie *Romeo and Juliet* had just opened. I thought the actress Olivia Hussey, who played Juliet, was the most beautiful girl in the world and I wanted to look exactly like her. She was the spokesgirl for Yardley cosmetics and so that's what I bought.

I chose a large, attractive container of loose powder. I remember the color was buff and it came with a big, soft black brush. I'm not sure what possessed me to buy loose powder, which is not a cosmetic tool any thirteen-year-old girl would ever need unless she was appearing onstage nightly in Las Vegas. When I put the powder on, it made me look as if I'd dredged my face in a bag of all-purpose flour. It didn't matter because I was not leaving the privacy of my bedroom, anyway. As much as I desperately wanted someone to notice me and think I was pretty, which is why I bought the makeup in the first place, I would die before I would let anyone see me with makeup on and have them know I cared about being pretty. Surely puberty was one of Dante's original rings of hell.

The fact that I never did get the hang of the loose powder, and wouldn't be caught dead in public with it on, anyway, didn't stop me from buying more makeup. Maybelline mascara, CoverGirl foundation, Bonne Bell lip gloss—whoever had the prettiest girl in their ad, that's the product I bought. I continued buying makeup, applying it in the privacy of my bedroom and washing it all off before anyone else could see it. My secret cosmetic life lasted more than a decade.

I went to college in my hometown, working as a carpenter in the university's theater and as a bartender in a "colorful" local tavern to put myself through school. I was offered a free ride out to New York and so I took it. I didn't know how to get into the stagehands' union and believed I wasn't good-looking enough to be a bartender in Manhattan, so I took a job as a live-in helper for a crippled ex-*Vogue* model. That's already too much said about that job.

Cindy, who was a highly skilled executive assistant, worked at the American Psychiatric Association. Luckily for me, she hated to do things alone, so she got me a job there, as well. We received great insurance perks on psychiatric care, so Cindy, who was already a fan of fasting, began to see a psychiatrist who gave her Optifast. It was the weight-loss plan du jour— even Oprah did it! Cindy lost thirty pounds on the fast and I gained twenty. The reason was that, to satisfy her intense food cravings, Cindy had taken to making me dinner almost every night. I was the only friend she had left who would let her stare at them while they ate. The food she made, while very eclectic, was not calorie conscious. I just didn't realize how fattening a meal of kielbasa, wild rice and peanut-butter-and-jelly sandwiches could be. I think it is safe to say that calorically I was very naive.

When the fast ended and Cindy had gained all her weight back plus more, she decided to fast again. Quitting my job wasn't an option and neither was gaining another twenty pounds, so

I fasted with her. We were two chubby women who believed they would never be beautiful or truly happy until they were thin, consuming only liquids while running the largest branch of the American Psychiatric Association. Wouldn't you have liked to have been a fly on that wall?

Not eating for two months was the most mind-numbing thing I've ever done. I was literally bored to tears on a daily basis. When Cindy, who was training to be an actress, started to take an improvisational comedy class to help "hone" her craft, she didn't have to work very hard to convince me to take it with her. Even though I had never harbored a single thought about being an actor, I jumped at the chance to do anything other than thinking about not eating.

Taking the class, as it turned out, was my salvation. In the improvisational skits I could become whoever I wanted so that when people looked at me, they weren't seeing me; they were watching an exotic belly dancer from Marrakesh or a bejeweled Marie Antoinette or a cowhand who had eaten too many beans. I felt completely at ease and comfortable onstage, whether playing a bewigged French beauty or someone sunburned and full of gas.

By now, again thanks to Cindy, we worked at the CBS Broadcast Center as secretaries. While we were there, another secretary named Bill Sherwood wrote a movie with a part in it for me. The movie opened in New York to great reviews, and after going to Los Angeles for the opening of the film, I found an agent, who began sending me out on auditions.

CROWN JEWEL

Every great dream begins with a dreamer. Always remember, you have within you the strength, the patience, and the passion to reach for the stars to change the world.
—Harriet Tubman

One day my agent sent me out on an audition for the part of someone who is applying for the job of selling cosmetics, but not only is she visually wrong for the job, she is the meanest, ugliest woman in the world. Well, to make a long story short, I got the job and it changed my life forever. I became Mimi on *The Drew Carey Show.*

At that moment everything that I had been running from my whole life hit me smack in the face—literally. I became the epicenter of cosmetics as we know it in the Western world. As Mimi, I wore more makeup on any one day than I had ever applied in all the years of my secret cosmetics obsession. And being looked at! It took place twenty-four hours a day. When I was dressed as Mimi and even when I was not. I became the object of intense scrutiny and attention. You know you're really in the public eye when you're standing in line at the grocery store and you see your picture on the front page of the *National Enquirer*. I'm just grateful the story wasn't about me having an alien's baby.

The truth is that this experience, which reeked to high heaven of irony, healed me like a miracle at Lourdes. Now, follow me here: the premise of the Mimi character was that in the eyes of society she was nightmare ugly but she didn't know it. Mimi thought she was not only beautiful but drop-dead sexy and gorgeous. For nine years I wore that vivid makeup, looked in the mirror and walked out of my dressing room, acting as if Mimi was beautiful, because that was my job—but in the "acting as if" I began to believe it. Within the first six months I would look in the mirror and think that Mimi was looking pretty good. By the end of the run of the show I believed with every fiber of my being that the character of Mimi was truly beautiful inside and out. By playing the meanest, ugliest woman in the world, I had discovered the means to help me be beautiful, the thing I had longed for all my life.

• • •

Wouldn't the ultimate gift to yourself be to believe that, no matter what your age, size or circumstances, you are beautiful and then go out into the world reflecting that feeling inside and out? It might be a lot easier to do if we understood that beautiful is a much more well-rounded idea than the simple meaning that our society has assigned to it. The dictionary definition of *beautiful* doesn't say anything about looking young, having no wrinkles or being thin. It says *beautiful* is having qualities that give great pleasure or satisfaction to see, hear or think about…

delighting the senses or mind; wonderful...very pleasing or satisfying; excellent of its kind; you.

Okay, we added *you* to the definition but it fits perfectly and that's the point. Beauty comes from the inside. Your naked face, gray hairs and softer body are beautiful just exactly the way they are because they tell the story of the life you've lived. Your laughter, struggles, courage and determination up until this point all combine to make a powerful source of energy within you that illuminates your face so that the world can see the remarkable story painted there.

Think about it this way. When you go to an art museum, you don't want to look at the same painting reproduced exactly the same way over and over again a thousand times. The enjoyment of visiting a museum is looking at the hundreds of works of art, each with the unique perspective of the individual artist. It's the delight in the details of each painting, the brushstrokes, and the colors and quality of light playing off one another that gives us pleasure. The same is true for us as women. Our unique experiences, wisdom, humor and compassion make us each an original work of art, perfect and beautiful just the way we are, and no more so than now in this second half of life.

WHAT WE DID TO FINALLY CLAIM OUR BEAUTY

We knew that not being able to see and understand how beautiful we were was just an outmoded habit we needed to break. We created an affirmation to help our brain replace the now-obsolete thought patterns. Our affirmation was "I am the sum of all my life experiences and I am beautiful beyond measure. I am ready to be the Queen of My Own Life—if not now, when?" We spoke it out loud every time we looked in the mirror. By really making eye contact with ourselves, not just a quick judging sweep of our face and body, we were able to start, one small step at a time, to reverse a lifetime of negative self-image. At first, it seemed a bit silly, but the more we repeated the affirmation the stronger and deeper we felt it.

When we weren't looking in the mirror, which was often, we used the deceptively simple but powerful tool of "acting as if." Which just meant that we *pretended* we thought we were beautiful. Whether out in the world dressed up, home in our pajamas, or in flip-flops, T-shirt and sweatpants, with dirty hair, pushing a shopping cart at the market, we were "acting as if" we were beautiful. In a surprisingly short amount of time it became the truth.

We felt the gradual transformation first in the relationship with our bodies. By acting as if we were beautiful, we actually began walking more confidently and it felt good. This new sassy walk acted as a signal to our brain that we were looking good, and we found that we began to crave that just like a "runner's high." The sassy walk to the mirror made the affirmation seem more true, and the truer the affirmation felt the sassier the walk got. This circle of sassy helped clear our vision and reset our reflections in the mirror. Our inner crone was banished and in its place stood two confident women who finally felt beautiful and were ready to be Queens.

HERE'S WHAT YOU CAN DO

We want this transformation for you, too. Please don't be afraid if it feels silly at first. We promise you it will get easier and soon seem more natural. There is a power in feeling beautiful that only you can give yourself and it's time to give yourself that gift.

Use our affirmation or create your own. Write it down on cards and tape it to every mirror in your house—even on the bottom of your rearview mirror in your car. When you look in the mirror, make eye contact with yourself and say the affirmation out loud every single time. This is important. Then act as if it's true, because it is. Walk the way you think a woman who knows she is beautiful would walk. There's no right or wrong way to do this. Our walk was sassy but maybe yours will be athletic or elegant. It doesn't matter, because it's whatever makes you feel beautiful. Then rinse and repeat. Seriously, keep affirming and "acting as if" and this gift will be yours.

Once you settle into feeling good about yourself, you'll be surprised by how well people will treat you. If you make the decision to be beautiful, you will be just that. It doesn't matter if you've been fired or someone walked out on you or you're struggling financially: you are beautiful and perfect just the way you are, and when you treat yourself royally, so will the rest of the world.

What will the second half of life write on your face? Hopefully it will be more joy, more adventure, perhaps some sorrow, but no matter what, it will be a pleasure to see, because the original work of art that is you grows more beautiful every day.

Here's a royal proclamation for you to read every day.

ROYAL PROCLAMATION

I am Queen of My Own Life and I shall
confront that damn talking mirror
every day. It will have no power over me.
Every time I look into it, I will see myself
as the beautiful, intelligent, valuable
woman that I am. So says the Queen.

CHAPTER 3

queen [kwēn] (noun) 1. a female ruler 2. an admired woman 3. the most powerful chess piece 4. a woman eminent in rank, power or attractions 5. a goddess or a female having supremacy in a specified realm

CLEAN YOUR MENTAL CLOSET AND FIND YOUR QUEEN VOICE

· · · *or* · · ·

Battling the Mongol Horde

Well done! You're acting as if you're beautiful, and fast becoming ruler over that damn magic mirror. Continue to practice until feeling beautiful becomes as natural as breathing. We promise you it will happen soon. Now it's time for you to clean your mental closet so you can find where you left your power.

Have you ever heard a voice inside of you say, "You're a wonderful person, and you're doing a fabulous job," or do you more often than not hear a voice that says things like, "What the hell were you thinking, you nitwit?" Well, the good news is that you're not going crazy. Everyone hears occasional negative and positive voices in their head. If your voices are always positive, put down this book and go buy a lottery ticket, because you are really lucky. But if far too often your voices are harsh or a bit cruel, like when you make a silly mistake and they say things like, "Good grief, come on—pay attention, you idiot!" or are more subtle and just cast doubt as in, "You could apply for a better job, but they'll never hire you, anyway, because you don't have enough experience," then by all means read on.

Have no fear, these voices are not the sign of adult-onset schizophrenia. We're pretty certain that everyone understands they're not really voices at all, but just very aggressive, negative thoughts. These unwanted thoughts are simply your own internal judgment inserting itself in such an intrusive, unsupportive way that it's like having a judge, a jury and the entire membership of the New York State Bar Association living rent-free in your head.

CROWN JEWEL

It is never too late to be what you might have been.

—George Eliot

Spending your valuable time listening to and trying to avoid hearing the negative voices crowding your brain gets in the way of living a fully productive and happy life. Somehow the intuitive voice, which when you were young told you to run, play, smile and have fun, has become buried under these harsh and judging voices. Uncovering your true voice, the voice of the Queen that still says to run, play, smile and have fun, is essential to claiming your throne.

Battling negative voices only you can hear can be a daunting task. To overcome them you could eat celery all day long—the crunching blocks all noise and thought—or you could wear headphones and crank your iPod up, which basically does the same thing as the celery but with more rhythm and variety. Ruling out the celery and iPod as being temporary fixes, we thought it best to give an identity to the voices so we could visualize what we were up against. We decided to call them the Mongol Horde. It seemed the perfect choice because, just like the voices in our heads, the Mongol Horde were wild, brilliant and unpredictable fighters with a take-no-prisoners policy. The battle cry of the Mongol Horde was said to strike terror in the hearts of all that heard it. With the action of naming the voices, we hoped not only to quiet them but change them from enemies to allies. Banishing the destructive Mongol Horde from our lives was definitely a battle worth waging and winning.

CROWN JEWEL

Fortunately, analysis is not the only way to resolve inner conflicts. Life itself still remains a very effective therapist.
—Karen Horney

KATHY

Before I was fortunate enough to land a job on *The Drew Carey Show,* I balanced working as a temporary secretary with working as a character actress. The acting jobs were few and far between and therefore quite precious. Once, I auditioned for and was thrilled to be hired to do a day's work on an extremely popular television show. I was delighted to have a job on a show that I enjoyed watching—the truth is that I was just plain overjoyed to have a job as an actor.

When I arrived at the studio that day, I went to hair and makeup and then waited on the set for the other actors. The show was on a studio lot that I had worked on before and I was pleased to recognize many people on the crew from a previous job. They were all as happy to see me as I was to see them and that made me feel good. Hollywood is the kind of place that can sap your self-esteem in the blink of an eye. Going to a job where I knew people and they knew me made it feel as if I belonged, like I was a real actor. The stars of the show finally arrived and we began rehearsing the scene.

Being a guest star on a long-running TV series is fraught with its own kind of peril. The regulars have been working together for a long time and are comfortable with one another and the characters they play. Very little rehearsal is required anymore as everyone has been doing it for so long, it's like a well-oiled machine. You, as the new cog in the machine, must come up to speed very quickly. Finding the tempo of the show and figuring out how to make your character fit in makes the job really fun and exciting. The atmosphere of the show is usually set by the graciousness and goodwill of the star. Most of the time you are treated with courtesy and respect. Sometimes, because actors are people, too, you are not treated very well, and that turned out to be the case on this show. By the time I finished work, after putting up with the stars' rude behavior all day, I not only felt that I didn't belong there but that they had made a huge mistake in hiring me in the first place. I was sure that by tomorrow the word would be out all over town that I had no talent at all.

CROWN JEWEL

**No one can make you feel inferior
without your consent.**

—Eleanor Roosevelt

As I got in my car to drive home that night, I could hear the Mongol Horde stamping their feet and rattling their spears, eager to make me feel worse than I already did. As someone who had been engaged in the "comparison game" since I was in junior high, I'd had many experiences with the Mongol Horde. As I put the car in gear, they let loose with a howl. "You idiot, what made you think you could act? You have no talent, never had a talent, never will have any talent!" Even as they were yelling at me, I thought to myself, "If I ever get on a show of my own, I'll make sure that everyone is treated with courtesy and kindness." I could barely keep the nasty voices in my head at bay and yet all I could do was think about someone else in the future.

By the time I got home I was a mess. The voices were so loud I almost couldn't catch my breath. Then a wonderful thing happened. I got angry. Usually I let the voices pummel me and scold me and I don't put up any kind of fight, because I believe they are telling me the truth. But that night I was tired and after a day of being treated badly by strangers, I was in no mood to be ill-treated by myself.

I went and got my kitchen timer and set it for ten minutes. I needed to prove to myself that no matter what the Mongol Horde threw at me, I could take it. I lay down on my bed and I said to those voices, "You've got ten minutes. If you can take me down, do it." Then I hit the start button on the timer. For ten merciless minutes, as I lay there, those voices tried every trick they knew to devastate me. "You're worthless, you're fat, you're stupid, you're ugly…nobody likes you…you have no talent, you'll never work again…your mother hates you, your father hated you, you'll never find love, you'll never be happy… you're a waste of space, you have no friends…"

The first few minutes were hard—the voices were sharp and almost evil—but then as the time went by the voices started to slow down and lose their power. They began to sound foolish and to say silly things, such as, "…and the cat hates you… and…and if you got another cat, that cat would hate you, too!"

I started to laugh. Then I sat up, turned off the timer and said, "Is that the best you've got? Because it's not good enough." I listened and there was silence—perfect, profound silence. I was filled with the same sense of calm and contentment that I've felt from cleaning a long-ignored and particularly messy closet. After discarding all the things I no longer needed there is so much more room for the truly important things. It felt so luxurious as I sat on the edge of the bed and savored my well-earned quiet.

I felt that the Mongol Horde was in full retreat but they could always regroup and mount another attack, so I laid down the rules: "From now on if you have nothing nice to say to me, then don't say anything at all. Instead of always trying to tear me down, I need you to support me." Again, only blissful silence, which I took as full agreement and surrender. I decided right then that I would be vigilant and never again fall into the trap of being the victim of my own negative self-judgment. Having the Mongol Horde as friends was going to be much more entertaining than battling them.

• • •

Never underestimate the Mongol Horde, because they are extremely clever and can transform themselves with the same skill as the greatest actress of our time—Meryl Streep (nominated for fifteen Academy Awards). Just when you learn to identify one of the negative voices and to ignore it, then it will simply change character. Sometimes a voice will be outright mean and loud, and other times so soft and quiet that you are left with just the feeling that someone has said something bad about you. However, the Mongol Horde's best battle tactic is the element of surprise. Sometimes even in the midst of being happy or pleased about your life, the Mongol Horde can sneak up and lob a low blow that can bring you to your knees, such as, "Sure, everything is good now but it's never going to last." With internal voices like these, who needs enemies?

CINDY

My Mongol Horde appeared recently after an especially challenging workweek. I'd been doing lots of writing that required concentration, research and focus, and frankly my brain was sore. I hadn't been out of the house in a couple of days, so I finally decided to go out and run some errands. I stopped at an ATM machine to get some cash and then went and filled up my car with gas. On the way home, suddenly, as if emerging from a blackout, I found that I had swerved across three lanes of traffic and was pulling into the Dunkin' Donuts parking lot and heading straight for the drive-through window.

As my vision began to clear, the Mongol Horde voices in my head were quietly chanting, "Dunkin' Donuts are good…. Dunkin' Donuts will change the way you feel." I hadn't realized my feelings needed to be changed. Out of the chorus of Mongol voices stepped one that was clear as a bell: "Powdered sugar isn't really very fattening at all." At this point I very faintly heard in the background my one lone voice of reason. "But sugar makes my heart beat too fast and makes my face flush." My honeyed Mongol voice assured me, "Such silly little reasons to deny yourself the pleasure of a sweet bite of yummy heaven."

Somehow I had the willpower to pull over and put the car in Park. I didn't have time for this and I certainly didn't need the extra calories. I'd promised myself just that morning that I'd eat healthfully that day. I'd gained ten pounds over the past year and I just didn't feel as good about myself as I used to.

Ever quick to grab an opening, the silver-tongued Mongol said, "BUT...you're doing so many things right. You exercise twice a week and you never did that before. You work so hard and you've accomplished so much this week. Surely you DESERVE a little treat. Here's a good idea. Don't buy the regular doughnuts. Just buy the Munchkins. They're so little and harmless and you DESERVE them."

I started to weaken. "Okay," I thought. "If I'm going to do this, at least I'll get the exercise of walking into the store and placing my order in person. I will not mindlessly drive through and then eat in the car. I'll go in." The Sir Laurence Olivier of the Mongols cooed, "Yes, good idea...you can diet tomorrow, because, really, you look fine. Who cares if you're carrying a few extra pounds? You're married.... It's not like you're out there trying to attract a husband. And besides, you have lots of flowy clothes that will cover the pooch.... Anyway, you DESERVE a little treat. Why not buy a whole box of the Munchkins? It's a better bargain and you can eat just one—really, you can—and then just save the rest for later."

As I started to get out of my car, I noticed something out

of the corner of my eye. A woman parked next to me in a Jeep Cherokee SUV was slithered down in her seat, drinking a tall cup of coffee and eating a powdered-sugar doughnut. She had a headband holding back her hair and looked as if she was wearing pajamas under her coat. She had that just-dropped-the-kids-off-at-school glazed look in her eyes and her vacant stare reminded me of exactly what I wanted to do—lose myself in a big cup of joe and a large mound of sugar…go to the happy place where nothing else was pulling at me, even if just for a moment.

I sighed to myself, looking across at my sugar twin, and thought, "Sister, I feel your pain. I know your stress." Then I noticed there were several other cars in the parking lot, all with their motors running. Each one harboring the same thing, woman after woman clutching coffee and doughnuts, taking a precious moment in a harried day just for themselves, attended by old friends—sugar, caffeine and the Mongol Horde.

I put the keys back in the ignition and drove out of the lot. I struck a compromise with the Mongols—I promised them and myself that if I still wanted a doughnut later, I'd come back. All I knew was at that moment I didn't want to be a part of the hollow-eyed pack of anxiousness that filled the cars in that parking lot. I didn't want to pay the price of a sugar high, sugar crash—regret and shame—that the pink-and-orange temple of Dunkin' Donuts represented. I needed to say, "Hey, I'm Queen of My Own Life, and for today I choose to take a long walk to relieve my stress. For today, I'm strong enough to banish the Mongol Horde and leave them lying in the Dunkin' Donuts parking lot."

CROWN JEWEL

**Life is not what it's supposed to be.
It's what it is. The way you cope with it
is what makes the difference.**

—Virginia Satir

As I pulled out into traffic I could hear the Mongol Horde gearing up to grumble, "Oh, great. You're still fat and ugly and you're not even going to get a doughnut? Nobody loves you. You really should get a doughnut, because doughnuts love you." Their foolish logic made me laugh, and the harder I laughed the quieter the voices became. They really hate to be laughed at. The voices remained quiet and I made it home safe and sugar-free.

Today, when I drive past Dunkin' Donuts, I still sometimes have the urge to go in. Instead, I just think of that day in the parking lot and my voices remain wonderfully quiet as I enjoy a good laugh at their expense. I like to think that I fought a great battle that day with the Mongol Horde. I call it the Battle of Doughnut Hill. It always makes me smile because I know I won a great victory that day.

• • •

Maybe it will help if you think about the situation this way. If you were constantly being criticized by a friend and every encounter with him or her left you feeling hurt, angry or doubtful about yourself, you'd quickly realize that you didn't want to spend time with them. If a stranger spoke harshly to you or called you names, you'd probably get angry and walk away. In these instances your sense of self-preservation would kick in and you'd find it easy to recognize that these were not good people for you to listen to or be near. You'd see very clearly that the negative things these people were doing or saying were harmful to you. You certainly wouldn't give them the power to determine how you felt about yourself. Why put up with the same behavior from the Mongol Horde that you would never allow from a friend or stranger? Although they reside in your head and are really only your own feelings of worry, self-doubt and fear, you must regard the Mongol Horde as an external threat to your well-being.

CROWN JEWEL

I was always looking outside myself for strength and confidence, but it comes from within. It is there all the time.

—Anna Freud

You can stop the Horde from ruling your life by naming them, laughing at them and demanding that they sign the Geneva convention and play fair. We have successfully learned to recognize an attack from the Mongol Horde and have become skilled at defending ourselves against their cunning ways by silencing them, and so can you.

WHAT WE DID TO BATTLE THE MONGOL HORDE

We were able to turn our Mongol Horde voices from enemies into allies. We acknowledged their existence, named them and learned to recognize them in all their subtle forms. Ultimately we did battle with them by finally confronting their lies. We brought out the big guns, and by using our secret weapon of laughter we were able to demand their unconditional surrender.

As we did this, sometimes we laughed and sometimes we felt sad and occasionally we were horrified to find out what terrible things we'd been saying to ourselves. But in the end we were able to really hear the voices and understand how truly wrong, and often hilarious, they were. The act of naming them, out loud, made them lose their power over us forever.

HERE'S WHAT YOU CAN DO

Let's go step-by-step through the exercise. You'll need a kitchen timer or any timer with an alarm. Find a quiet place where you can be alone and focus on your thoughts. Set the timer for ten minutes. It's important to give yourself ten full minutes and not rush this exercise because, as we've said be-fore, the Mongol Horde can be very wily. It's our experience that they're also impatient, so by allowing yourself ten full minutes of quiet contemplation we think you'll be surprised by the powerful act of simply declaring that you're worth the time investment.

For us, it was powerful to lie down on our beds because it made us feel vulnerable and helped us get in touch with our in-ner thoughts. But sitting in a comfortable chair or cross-legged on the floor can work just as easily. The point is to be alone with yourself and the negative thoughts.

Speaking out loud, tell the Mongol Horde, "I have set aside ten minutes to hear all the negative things you have to say about me. So, give it your best shot, and if you think you can take me down, go ahead and try it. Because after that ten min-utes is up, I will not allow you to speak to me AT ALL unless you can be supportive." Start the timer and relax. At first you might find yourself thinking, "Gosh, this is silly. I'm talking to myself and I don't have anything to say back." But you com-mitted to giving yourself ten minutes, so stay still and think about the negative messages you've been hearing.

As these messages begin to come to mind, go ahead and say them out loud, as though the Mongol Horde is speaking. Giving voice to the negative thoughts will help you hear how truly foolish and untrue they are. As the timer bell rings, say to the voices, "Is that the best you can do? Because it's not good enough." Then in your most royal declarative voice give them their new marching orders as follows: "These things you've been saying about me are not true. I do not accept them and will no longer listen to you, Mongol Horde. Your new job is to say only kind, loving and supportive things to and about me from now on."

We realize that the Mongol Horde will likely always be lurking somewhere. But now that you've cleaned out your mental closet they won't be able to trick you into listening to them. You can always use your newfound Queen voice to laugh at them and send them running in retreat. Isn't that a great gift for a Queen to give herself?

ROYAL PROCLAMATION

Hear ye, hear ye, Academy Award–winning
voices of the Mongol Horde. If you don't have
anything good to say to me, then don't say
anything at all. I banish all your negative
and nasty talk. I, the Queen, decree it and so
it shall be from this day forward.

CHAPTER 4

admire [ad'mī(ə)r] (verb) 1. regard with wonder, delight and pleased approval 2. marvel at 3. treasure 4. be in awe of 5. respect 6. have a high opinion of 7. look up to 8. think the world of

ADMIRE YOURSELF FOR WHO YOU'VE BECOME

. . . or . . .

Your Windy Mountain Moment

Hurray! You've successfully cleaned your mental closet and there on the bottom, underneath a bunch of old dented Mongol Horde shields, a few broken spears and some really smelly fur boots, you found your Queen voice. The Mongol Horde may occasionally return for the boots, so you will have to remind them that you've given them new marching orders and they are now your allies. But, with a clean closet, it's time to claim the next gift—admiring yourself for who you've become.

Remember the old analogy of life being a tapestry? We believe that's true, but we think that most of the time we live at the back of the tapestry, where it's all messy, with knots and strings hanging everywhere, and we're just jumping around trying to avoid the sharp needle that keeps poking through. It's a rare moment when we get to step around to the front and take in the beauty of a life well lived.

Taking the time to stop and look back at where you've come from is an important opportunity for personal insight that we call a Windy Mountain Moment. As if you were standing on top of a beautiful mountain with a clean wind blowing, you look back over your life and reflect on the amazing journey you've been on to date and the really good job you did of getting here. Somewhere along the way on this journey, you've developed a great set of survival skills that have brought you to the top of this mountain with your hairdo being rearranged by the wind. We discovered at our original Crowning Ceremony we needed to take time to not only acknowledge our incredible journey but to admire what expert travelers we have become.

·· CROWN JEWEL ··

**What a wonderful life I've had!
I only wish I'd realized it sooner.**

—Colette

Who is the last woman you admired—Oprah, Angelina Jolie, Wonder Woman as played by Linda Carter? Have you ever admired yourself? Isn't it about time to add yourself to the list? The language you use to describe your journey and experiences affects how you view yourself and how others view you. It's crucial to use words that are positive and life affirming in order to give yourself and others permission to admire you.

In life everyone has some sadness or regrets over chances lost and mistakes made, or what we call the "could've, would've, should'ves." Sometimes as we climb up the mountain we wear this sadness and regret like a big old damp wool coat. We've worn it so long that we might not even notice it anymore, but when meeting others it's the first thing they see. Wearing this outdated regret and sadness affects how we feel about ourselves and how others perceive us.

Stopping high up on this mountain, where the air is clear, you will be able to look back and see what traits you want to banish that aren't working and what ones you want to keep and polish up in order to become the kind of Queen you can admire. Ultimately it's up to you to choose the attributes your Queen will have in this second half of your journey. We think you already have all the qualities you need to be a spectacular Queen. We're going to guide you to the top of the mountain so you can name them, claim them and dress them up in new language—and you can finally give yourself the admiration you have earned.

CROWN JEWEL

**One is not born a woman,
one becomes one.**
— Simone de Beauvoir

KATHY

I loved my father dearly, and as his only child I believe he adored me. When I was very little I couldn't wait for him to come home from work. My world felt safe and complete with him in the house.

When I was five years old my father's health worsened and, due to his smoking and conditions on his job, he was diagnosed with chronic bronchial asthma. Over the next ten years, as his lungs deteriorated, they began to call it emphysema.

Unable to breathe, he was also unable to work, and we were soon living on Social Security disability. When I was fifteen, he died, and even though he had been sick for ten years, it seemed very sudden. I was devastated.

As a minor I continued to receive a check each month from Social Security. Through the rest of high school I spent most of my time grieving and really didn't give much thought to what I wanted to do once I had graduated.

A couple of weeks after graduation I was standing in a bar with my friends, drinking a beer (back then the drinking age was actually eighteen—what were they thinking?). One of my friends anxiously asked, "What are we going to do now that we're done with high school?" I remember taking a swig of beer and replying very matter-of-factly, "Go to vocational school and become licensed practical nurses." She nodded her head okay. The decision was made and the next day we went to fill out applications and get fitted for our uniforms.

That night I sat in my bedroom, and for the first time since my father died I thought about what I really wanted my life to be like when I grew up. From the time I was five years old, and had been given a View-Master with a three-disk set of the Wonders of the World, I had wanted to travel. I would stare at those disks, clicking away, and imagine myself in Paris, looking at the Eiffel Tower; in China, standing on the Great Wall; or in Pisa, standing with arms akimbo, gazing at the Leaning Tower.

While growing up I spent many happy summer hours in the public library, reading stories about girls who went off to college. They had lovely wardrobes and in their junior year they went abroad to faraway places, where they became fluent in beautiful romance languages and met dreamy foreign boys. When they came home, they graduated from college and moved to big cities where they got large apartments, exciting friends and interesting jobs. In none of my books or dreams did the heroine drink beer, stay put in her hometown and become a licensed practical nurse.

When I turned eighteen, I received a letter from the Social Security office telling me that as long as I was in school, I would continue to receive a monthly payment until the end of the semester I turned twenty-one. As I sat in my bedroom that night I realized that, even though I didn't have a lovely wardrobe, I wanted to go to college more than anything in the world. The next morning I called my friend and told her that I'd changed my mind and I wouldn't be going to vocational school with her. She went on to take the classes and became a warm and caring LPN, a job she still holds to this day.

> **The question isn't who is going to let me;**
> **it's who is going to stop me.**
>
> —Ayn Rand

I went to college and my junior year I spent a semester in London. While there I went to Paris and saw the Eiffel Tower and I've been lucky enough to go back many times since. I've been to China and walked on the Great Wall and I've been to Pisa and leaned on the Leaning Tower. I've traveled from Romania to Iraq and to many countries in between. I still love to travel and do it as often as I can.

After college I moved to New York and eventually to Los Angeles. I still have friends from my hometown and from college that I hold dear, as well as beloved friends I made while living in New York. I've had many interesting jobs and met many dreamy foreign boys. The only thing I never did was become fluent in a beautiful romance language, but it certainly isn't from lack of trying, and I still have hope that it may happen someday.

I'm not telling you this story to make you feel sorry for me, although in years gone by I might have wanted that. Through my youth I did define myself by the sad experience of losing my father. Being young, and without a lot of guidance, I hadn't learned how to process grief yet. As the years went by and other events occurred in my life, I added to the definition of me. I sorted through these events and labeled them good and bad. I found it much easier to define myself by the drama and sadness of the "bad" events rather than enjoy the positive feelings from the "good." Even as I was maturing and becoming successful, inside I was still poor, fatherless Kathy.

My Windy Mountain Moment came on set one day while shooting a TV show. I was having lunch with a few of the other actors and someone mentioned that, what with the sad state of the Social Security Administration today, by the time we were old enough to retire, we wouldn't be able to receive benefits because there wouldn't be any money left. I told them that I was okay with that and explained how I had received Social Security benefits while I was in college because of my father's death. I barely had the sentence out of my mouth before my whole life flashed in front of my eyes. The money I had received to go to college came because my father had died—those payments had altered the course of my life, and without them, I wouldn't be where I was and who I was today.

Standing on top of that windy mountain and looking back over my life, I saw that from that "bad" experience had come all these amazing opportunities. While more than anything I would rather have my father alive and in good health, I would not be the woman I am today with so many of my dreams fulfilled if it were not for that experience forcing my life to change direction. With the feeling of a cool breeze on my face I looked at all the other events in my life that I had labeled as "bad" and I saw that from each of those experiences my life had jogged in a different and eventually more beneficial way. I saw the zigs and zags of my life laid out behind me and I had no regrets. I thought the pattern that they made was unique and beautiful. Now, instead of labeling events in my life, I choose to believe that there is indeed a positive purpose in all things. And I no longer define myself as poor, fatherless Kathy but instead think of myself as successful, happy, grateful Kathy, who is looking forward to climbing even taller mountains.

• • •

Wouldn't it be interesting to look back at the experiences you've had in your life without labeling and without judgment? If you take the time to review your life, you'll notice that good things often came from "bad" experiences and sometimes bad things from "good." A Queen has no time to be a victim or regret things that happened to her when she was nine years old or twenty-five or even from some lapse in judgment that happened yesterday. It's time to throw away that damp wool coat and let go of the old events that you've been using to define yourself. And as you come closer to the top of the mountain, why not slip on a nice waterproof windbreaker and get ready to create new language to describe what kind of Queen you want to be?

CINDY

The company I worked for recently eliminated my job and after eleven years I was unceremoniously let go. To be honest, there had been hints for more than a year that something like this might happen, but I kept telling myself that if I just put my head down, worked harder and ignored the signs, I would survive the next round of cuts. I was wrong. I was hurt, humiliated and angry.

Ironically, I wasn't happy at this job and hadn't been for a long time. Still, the actual moment I was let go felt like a kick in the stomach, and the hurt didn't seem to lessen. In fact, it grew worse as I came to realize just how much of my self-esteem had been attached to my job title and what I did for a living.

CROWN JEWEL

**Life is a process of becoming,
a combination of states we have to go
through. Where people fail is that
they wish to elect a state and remain in it.
This is a kind of death.**

—Anaïs Nin

In my newly unemployed moments, I just couldn't hang on to feeling good about myself. It was as though I suddenly, overnight, had gone from being a respected and intelligent businesswoman to a gypsy con artist who was afraid people would discover she was a fraud. I felt ashamed because I thought others would think I hadn't been smart enough, or the company would have wanted to keep me. A strategic business decision by my former employer felt like a personal judgment of my value and worth as a person. I just couldn't shake those been-let-go blues.

Over and over in my head, I played back every career decision I'd made in the past few years and was filled with regret that I hadn't done something earlier. Why hadn't I changed jobs when I first noticed the company was struggling? I wasted many weeks feeling angry, sorry for myself and embarrassed.

About a month after being let go I got a call from an out-placement service reminding me that my layoff package included their support and resources. I hadn't yet been over to meet them because I was still struggling with my hurt pride. They let me know that an upcoming workshop with a résumé specialist might be an excellent way to sample their services and move forward. I hadn't put together a résumé in more than a decade and realized that I needed the extra kick in the pants to get this basic task done, so I signed up.

On the first day of the workshop we were told we'd need to share our current résumé. I quickly created one using a standard format, listed all my jobs and responsibilities and returned to my coach for advice. I expected her to be impressed with my level of experience and tell me I had a fine résumé. Instead, I was stunned to learn that I'd written a very average description of myself. She went on to talk about the importance of using powerful, dynamic language that would bring my résumé to the top of the pile and help me stand out from the crowd with prospective employers.

The coach pointed out that the words I'd used in my résumé, like *supervised* and *responsible for,* were dull and didn't do anything to highlight my accomplishments. She asked me to put down the résumé and describe my job experiences to her. As I started talking about all the exciting projects and programs I'd been involved with, I became very animated. The coach listened to me and then shared what she observed, that I obviously had loved the work I'd done, been energized by it and really had a passion for it. She then showed me how to enhance my language with words like *conceived, executed, developed, pioneered, motivated* and *created.* I could actually feel the pride in my accomplishments growing as I used this new language to describe my career.

I had never heard of an executive summary before, but now I was told that I needed one. She said it was a brief, to-the-point paragraph summing up my work experiences by using appealing key words that would catch a potential employer's attention. She explained that more often than not employers don't even read résumés anymore. They simply scan the executive summary for key words that help them to focus on the best job applicants.

During my years in communications and marketing I'd won awards for creative campaigns touting other people's talents, but here I was, baffled at how to do the same for myself. Boiling down a twenty-plus-year career into one brief paragraph and pinning my future employment on just a few words was frightening. As happens with most scary things, once I let go of my fear of failure and focused on the task, writing the paragraph turned out to be a great life-changing exercise.

CROWN JEWEL

> **When one door closes, another opens; but we often look so long and so regretfully upon the closed door that we do not see the one which has opened for us.**
> —Alexander Graham Bell

As I tackled the assignment, I was also letting go of the hurt and anger that had been holding me captive during the past month. The exercise of describing my accomplishments helped me see clearly who I had been and who I had become. By retracing my work history, focusing on the accomplishments I was most proud of and then searching for more dynamic words to describe the talents and skills I had developed, I was able to rewrite my executive summary and my personal story in a positive and energetic way.

Yet, when my résumé came back from the printer I took it out of the envelope and could only stare at it. There, in bold black ink, was a brief but very powerful description of a clever, gifted woman who would be an asset to any company that would hire her. Surely this paragraph couldn't be about me. If I had been this amazing, wouldn't I still be employed? I felt like such a fraud.

As I paced around my home office I practiced saying aloud, "I'm an experienced and talented executive." Now, I felt like I was bragging and nice girls don't brag, do they? The truth was that I had achieved all the things I'd listed on my résumé but I was afraid that someone might read it and say, "Well, she sure thinks a lot of herself." As I circled around my desk one more time I began to wonder why it wasn't okay for me to shine. I wasn't bragging. All these things were accurate descriptions of me.

At different times through the day I would stop and reread my executive summary. It was a wonderful description of an accomplished woman with so much to offer. This was a woman I wanted to work side by side with and who would hopefully be my friend. This was a woman with qualities I could admire. I have to admit I had to read that paragraph nine or ten times before I could finally begin to accept that the woman being described there was me.

As I stood there holding my résumé, looking back at my past history, I had a Windy Mountain Moment. Reading the language my résumé coach had encouraged me to use opened my eyes and helped me see myself as she did—not as someone who had been set aside, but as someone who had a great deal of experience and value. That moment when I finally gave myself permission to believe the powerful new language that she had helped me create was when my anger and hurt finally began to dissipate. Embracing this new description of myself allowed me to see that life was full of many new opportunities and to begin to feel excited about what lay ahead.

Soon after standing on top of that windy mountain, I started my own consulting company and began writing a book, giving workshops and taking new classes. I was literally set free by creating a new me anchored in the wonderful old me that I had rediscovered. The challenge of describing myself in new dynamic phrases gave me the clarity and finally the courage to admire myself. And it all came from being fired. I wonder if I should send my old company a thank-you card?

• • •

Look, we understand that everyone has both challenges and successes on their climb up the mountain. We all have to deal with illness, death, loss of jobs, divorce and money woes. The trick is in not letting yourself be defined as a victim of these events. Stop trying to put labels on your life and definitions on yourself. It's easier than you think. It takes only one good Windy Mountain Moment.

CROWN JEWEL

Adventure is worthwhile in itself.
—Amelia Earhart

Try thinking of it like this: you have been steadily climbing up a steep mountain that is densely covered with shrubs and trees. The path has so many twists and turns, it's hard to see where you've been and where you're going. Occasionally there are large boulders blocking your way. Sitting down, waiting for the boulder to miraculously move while you weep, "Why me!" is one option. Or another way to handle it is to find a new path around the boulder and continue your climb up the mountain with the understanding that the boulder is neither good nor bad but simply a boulder. Just when the path becomes the steepest and you're not sure you can go on, you suddenly come out of the trees onto the top of the mountain and the view is incredible. Around you are the peaks of other mountains that you will soon climb. But for now, as a crisp, clean wind refreshes you and raises hell with your hair, turn around to see spread behind you, in all its clarity, the path that you've just been on.

WHAT WE DID TO LEARN TO ADMIRE OURSELVES

Having a Windy Mountain Moment is an important life-altering experience that can occur from any number of catalysts in life. While ours happened spontaneously, we'll soon show you the steps to take to create your own. Our WMMs helped us realize that we were giving off outdated verbal signals to ourselves and others about who we were and what we thought about ourselves. We needed to spruce up our language to reflect who we had really become and what kind of Queen we wanted to be.

We started by making a list of women that we admired. This list ranged from women like Mother Teresa and Amelia Earhart to friends, neighbors and family members. Then we went over the list and wrote down the virtues that we most valued in these women, such as kind, faithful, bold, smart, generous, hopeful, brave, loyal, gentle, loving, poised, strong, independent. When the list was complete we read them out loud slowly. We narrowed the list down to the four we responded to most strongly, which were generous, loving, kind and brave.

Then we asked each other a very difficult question: "What qualities do you like best in yourself?" For many women, answering this question does not come naturally. Even now it can be uncomfortable for a woman to toot her own horn. We had a few false starts with, "I think I'm a good mother," or "I think I'm a first-rate friend." What we really wanted were the qualities that we like about ourselves that made us good mothers and friends. When we were finally able to voice what we liked about ourselves, we wrote down these attributes. And when we compared them to the list of the top four virtues we most admired in other women, we discovered that they were the same. We had always been the kind of women that we could admire but somehow we had lost sight of that in the chaos of climbing the mountain.

We decided that these four words—*generous, kind, loving and brave*—would be great for our coat of arms. After all, every Queen needs one. Putting these words on our own personal coat of arms and looking at it every day serves as a reminder to us of the power of language to transform the way we feel about ourselves and the way we want the world to view us. Now it's your turn.

HERE'S WHAT YOU CAN DO

Here's how you can create your own Windy Mountain Moment. Close your eyes and imagine that you're standing on top of a high mountain and the wind is blowing. (If you've got a fan, and it helps, turn it on low.) Look back over the first half of your life. Quick, choose the moment that you've come to think of as the most difficult or that most altered the course of your life. Now, letting go of the "could've, would've, should'ves," allow yourself to see how this experience is just a large boulder that you needed to get around. Try thinking of it as the universe's way of putting up a big road sign that says Road Closed—Turn Left Now.

Now, get a piece of paper and pen. Write down the ten women you admire most. Then list the qualities that you most value in these women. Read them out loud slowly. It might help to look in a mirror while you do this. Put a check or star next to the four words that resonate the most strongly for you. Now—and you knew this was coming—what qualities do you like best in yourself? Don't be afraid—this isn't bragging; it's a private conversation between you and you. So, go for it. Compare the two lists. Are there any words on the lists that match? If there are, chances are good these words are core values for you. If none of them match, don't worry; it's all a process and in the end you get to choose the four you most want your Queen to be. And, at different times in your life, any or all of these words can change, so don't get hung up on being perfect in this.

On page 160 you will find a blank coat of arms. Make a copy of it, or write your four words or virtues right in the book, and rip the page out, or you can go to our Web site (www.queenofyourownlife.com) and download a coat-of-arms template to decorate to your heart's content. The point is to make one and keep it where you can see it.

When you're finished with your coat of arms, face the fan and read the four words out loud with gusto. Now to the bottom of the page add *I admire this woman, I admire me* and sign your name. We admire you, too. It's been a remarkable journey and you're going to make a wonderful Queen.

ROYAL PROCLAMATION

Let it be known from this day forward that I have conceived, executed, developed, pioneered, motivated and created an extraordinary life and I will speak about myself in a positive way from this moment on because I am worth it. I give you permission to admire me even as I take time every day to admire myself. So sayeth the Queen.

CHAPTER 5

support [səpôrt] (verb) (noun) 1. keep something or somebody stable 2. give active help and encouragement 3. give assistance or comfort 4. enable someone to live 5. help in crisis 6. give courage, faith or confidence to

BUILD DEEP,
FULFILLING FRIENDSHIPS
WITH OTHER WOMEN

. . . or . . .

Choosing Your Court

You've *motivated* yourself to develop new language to describe your life's journey. Then you *created* a lovely personal coat of arms using this active life-affirming language so that you can remember that you are worthy of your own admiration every time you look at it. Now it's time for you to *pioneer* a way to fill your life with positive, trustworthy women who will help you reign supreme.

If you do an Internet search for Paris Hilton's BFF (best friend forever), you'll get 1,090,000 responses. That's a lot of best friends, and by the time you're done reading this paragraph, we're sure the number will have grown. It's nice to have a lot of friends but we're talking about building and nurturing that small core of trusted women you rely on for life support—we call them your agenda-free Ladies-in-Waiting, or your LIW.

We believe that everybody needs someone they trust to watch them live so that, on occasion, they can ask them, "How am I doing?" and know they will get an honest answer. We're not talking about that friend or family member who is always so quick to criticize or give you unsolicited advice on what to wear, how to style your hair or when to discipline your kids. We're talking about that very good friend or friends who are always available to listen to your problems without trying to solve them. Someone who supports you, but is not afraid to lovingly tell you when you're off base, and has no hidden agenda about your friendship. She just wants the best for you.

Think about the women in your life. Is your support system just that—a support system—or do you have women in your life who undermine you? Do you have someone in your life who would be unhappy if you changed? Someone who would not like it if you, say, lost weight, stopped drinking, went back to school, got a divorce or moved to Kansas City? Spending time with someone who is competitive with you or who you simply share a bad habit with might not be a basis for a good friendship.

Have you ever been afraid to tell your close friends something that you were thinking about or wanted to do because you were afraid that they would judge you? You should be able to talk to your LIW without fear. Friendships are meant to be safe, enriching and full of love and lots of laughter. Do you have this kind of bond in your life? Having a strong support system is essential. We're not saying dump all your friends;

we're just saying take a look at who you rely on. Are you getting what you need from these relationships?

CROWN JEWEL

A friend is someone who knows the song in your heart and can sing it back to you when you have forgotten the words.

—Unknown

Of course, the place to start is with your own behavior. Are you a good Lady-in-Waiting to your friends, or do you judge their behavior and then gossip behind one another's backs, making little tsk-tsk noises and shaking your head over how they live their lives? It's really simple—if you don't want to be judged, then don't judge anyone else. Our Queen is loving, honest, generous and brave. In our friendships we act the Queen and we look to surround ourselves with women who do the same. We believe that the best gift you can give yourself, as the Queen, is to surround yourself with a court of trusted advisers: your own inner circle of Ladies-in-Waiting.

CINDY

When I got engaged, I asked Kathy and my sisters, Pam and Lee Ann, to be in my wedding party. I also asked my friend

"Jean Marie." I'd been her maid of honor the year before, when she married my ex-boyfriend, Mark. It was New York in the early '80s and we were theater people, which, if you'd been there, would explain everything. But suffice it to say that Mark and I had been college sweethearts and had lived together in New York for years, and although our couplehood ended in a dramatic and messy fashion, our friendship survived. So being maid of honor at his wedding was as much an act of friendship for Mark as it was for Jean Marie.

Kathy, my sisters and Jean Marie all said yes and we began the whirlwind task of planning my wedding, which was only six months away. Jean Marie was a dancer and performing in her very first Broadway show, a big, brassy tap-dancing extravaganza that was the toast of Broadway at the time. She was in the chorus and understudying one of the leads and it was all very glamorous.

In the two years Jean Marie had been in the show, she'd never taken a vacation day and that fact was a source of pride for her. Vacation days are written into the contracts and the cast is entitled to use them but she never did. Yet she assured me that she would do so for my wedding and told me she had submitted an official request for an approved vacation day.

I know you've seen this coming since the start of the story, so here it is…. Literally two weeks (thirteen days to be exact) before the wedding, she told me that her producers hadn't approved her vacation request and she could not get the day of my wedding off and couldn't be in the wedding party.

Enter Cynthia. I called Cynthia, who I had been working

with for four years in our improvisational comedy group, and asked her to fill in for Jean Marie. Now, you'd think that a last-minute invitation to be a bridesmaid, knowing you weren't first choice and having to make do with someone else's dress, would offend or hurt feelings. But bless her heart, Cynthia accepted and jumped into the preparations and festivities with enthusiasm. She never once hinted that she felt slighted at not being first choice. She was supportive, fun, joyous and, by God, she looked good in what I now believe were the ugliest bridesmaid dresses ever seen on the East Coast. Also, she doesn't hold it against me that, to this day, she still has a small scar on her forehead from the scuffle that broke out when I tossed my bouquet.

CROWN JEWEL

Grief can take care of itself; but to get the full value of a joy you must have somebody to divide it with.

—Mark Twain

I was disappointed and hurt Jean Marie dropped out of my wedding but I'm grateful for the way things turned out. In the twenty-six years I have known Cynthia, she has shown me, over and over, exactly what an intelligent, strong, caring woman and friend she is. She has always offered me unconditional love and support and I strive to be able to offer her the same in return. Despite being separated by distance, she serves as a regal member of my trusted inner court. I value her opinion and counsel highly and feel very fortunate to have her in my life.

• • •

Some women have very strong, healthy friendships within their families. It's a great gift to have a sister, cousin, mother or aunt you can rely on for encouragement and support. Having been in your life for a long time, they know exactly what a wonderful child you were and what an amazing woman you've grown into. Not every woman is that lucky, but it's also an incredible gift to be able to choose your friends and create a handpicked family of strong, caring women who you can rely on for guidance, loyalty and hope.

KATHY

My parents were married for thirteen years before they finally had me. Although I appeared to be a robust child, I was often ill due to the fact that I was born allergic to all dairy products. It being Wisconsin, everyone told my mother to just give me some skim milk and low-fat cottage cheese and I'd be fine. Which is exactly what she did and which is why for my entire childhood I had a chronic ear infection, red, swollen tonsils, a head full of snot and a stiff handkerchief printed with images of "kittens who had lost their mittens" in my pocket.

As the story goes, when I was three years old and the weather was nice, which was about six days out of the year, my parents would put me in a playpen out in the backyard. I believe the theory was that the sun would heal me by melting the snot right out of me. Of course, that never happened but I did get a face covered with freckles that have now turned into lovely age spots, and I got something else. One day they found another three-year-old girl standing outside the playpen, staring at me through the bars. She had followed her older brothers, who had come over to play with the kids next door. Her name was Cindy and she became the "First Cindy" in my life and my very first best friend.

CROWN JEWEL

Each friend represents a world in us, a world possibly not born until they arrive, and it is only by this meeting that a new world is born.

—Anaïs Nin

The First Cindy and I spent our childhood playing games and having fun. We would sit in my sandbox for hours, pretending to make cakes, or we would swing on the swing set, imagining ourselves flying off to exotic locations, like France or Milwaukee. We ate teeny tiny crab apples off the tree in her backyard and spent hours lying on an old army blanket in my front yard, playing with the Betsy McCall paper dolls I had cut out of my mother's magazines. We created a world together where every moment was an enjoyable adventure, as well as a place where we were safe no matter what was going on around us.

Cindy was able to go to kindergarten first because her birthday was in June and I had to wait because mine was in November. I used to ride my tricycle to the corner every day to wait for her to come home from school. By now they'd taken out my poor tortured tonsils in an attempt to cure me of the chronic earaches. To keep the cold Wisconsin wind from blowing through my sore ears, my mother always tied a giant head scarf on me before letting me out of the house. So every weekday I would sit on my tricycle, waiting for Cindy, with my thick scarf tied under my chin, looking like the inner piece of a set of those hand-painted Russian stacking dolls.

The First Cindy and I stayed best friends until she went off to the sophisticated world of junior high. Then the rule about the older kids not hanging out with the younger kids kicked in and we soon went our separate ways.

I started hanging out with another girl from our neighborhood who was a bit younger than me and, oddly enough, also named Cindy. The "Second Cindy" and I spent a lot of fun hours making tents on her mother's clothesline from old blankets, playing with our Barbie dolls and running wild in the cemetery day and night, trying to scare each other silly. I stayed best friends with her until I went off to the sophisticated world of junior high and, well, you know, that old rule kicked in.

**Friendship is when people know
all about you but like you anyway.**

—Unknown

In high school I occasionally saw the First Cindy in the hall but we rarely spoke. Most of my friends now were named Kathy, so we called one another by our last names to avoid confusion. Then, in my sophomore year, in the very early hours of a spring day, my father passed away. That morning, as my mother sat in her bedroom and I sat in mine, trying to process the enormity of our grief and unable to comfort each other, there was a knock at our front door. When I opened it, there stood the First Cindy. I remember it was a school day and I was so surprised to see her. I said, "What are you doing here?" She looked startled that I was surprised and simply said, "Your dad died...I'm here to spend the day with you." So I let her in and that's what she did. For that whole day, in spite of my sadness, I again felt the comfort and safety of the world we had created together. She revealed herself that day to be the kind of woman she would grow up to be and the kind of friend I would cherish forever.

Cindy Ratzlaff (the "Third Cindy") and I met one summer while in college, when we were in a play together called

The Boy Friend by Sandy Wilson. Cindy had an ingenue role, Hortense the maid, and I played old Lady Brockhurst, who simply wandered the stage occasionally calling for her philandering husband, Hubert. The director cast me because he didn't have anyone else to play the role. He saw me every day because I had a work-study job in the scene shop of the theater department and I guess he figured as long as I was already there, he might as well use me. I had never been in a play before, had never thought about being an actor and had no idea what was expected of me onstage. In a foreshadowing of my days to come on *The Drew Carey Show* I found out I was expected to dance.

During the curtain call we were all supposed to do the Charleston as the big finale. I would hide in the back row during rehearsals, desperately trying to learn the steps. They just wouldn't stick in my nondancer brain. At the dress rehearsal the director set the finale and put me right in the front row. I was terrified. On opening night the play went off without a hitch and suddenly we were into the big finale. As the music for the Charleston started, I froze. The actor on my right, a very talented man by the name of Kerry Schussler, took pity on me and started calling out, "Left foot, now right foot, now your left!" By following his directions, I found myself finally doing the Charleston and I was overjoyed. Once I had the dance, I threw myself into it with wild abandon. I had no idea the audience had been watching the whole thing and were roaring with laughter at what they thought was a great comic bit.

After the show the director came up to me in the green room, stared at me and then blurted out that he had no idea why everyone was laughing so hard at my character during the curtain call. As I said, I hadn't realized they were laughing at me, so I had no answer for him. I never did figure out how to just start dancing the Charleston on my own, so I continued to "accidentally" steal the curtain call every night with the help of Kerry, who had the sense and comic timing to turn it into a wonderful stage moment for us both.

One night, partway through the run, Cindy came up to me as we were putting on our makeup and asked me if I had gotten the note from the director telling me that I was no longer in the curtain call, and then she laughed. She's always amazed when I say that at that moment I thought she was a real bitch. She says she thought she was being hilarious and I simply didn't get her dry, sophisticated wit, which she had acquired that one year she lived in Minneapolis.

After we left college, we both eventually ended up in New York. Our paths crossed often as we socialized in a large group of our college friends who had all moved to New York to make it big in theater. We spent many evenings engaged in the Wisconsin sport of sitting in bars, drinking, solving the world's problems and playing foosball. As we saw each other almost every weekend, Cindy and I eventually began a casual, easy friendship.

CROWN JEWEL

Friendship with oneself is all-important, because without it one cannot be friends with anyone else in the world.
—Eleanor Roosevelt

As I told you before, Cindy hated to do things by herself and had easily convinced me to take a comedy improvisation workshop with her. The thing about improvisational comedy is that it's so fun, it can be very addictive. So, once you learn the skill of improvisation, you need a place to use it. Cindy and several of the women from the workshop decided to start an all-women's improvisation and sketch comedy group and perform at clubs around the city. Of course, Cindy included me in the plan.

For the first few years we performed together it was an unruly democracy at best. There were five of us and we were young, often hormonally unbalanced and had a tendency to bicker over every little detail of running the group—and there were a lot of details. We wrote the sketches, booked the venues and created and mailed out the flyers to our friends, who became the invited audiences that paid a cover price and a two-drink minimum just to watch us. We also designed our own costumes—a hot-pink blouse and black pants, which in retrospect made us look more like an exhibition bowling team than a professional comedy group. In spite of all that, we managed to create some very funny material that I'm still proud of to this day.

After five years, relationships in the group really started to go downhill. We still hadn't achieved the level of fame and world domination that we had been hoping for. Tempers were set on hair triggers, and in truth, names were called and feelings were hurt. We finally decided to get a director to take charge because we were no longer able to see clearly what needed to be done.

The director we turned to knew us all and was an old friend of mine. As it worked out, the decision to involve her was the best idea we had ever had. Not because she smoothed out our rough edges and made us better performers, which she did, but because she helped Cindy and me cement our friendship forever.

CROWN JEWEL

I believe the greatest gift I can conceive of having from anyone is to be seen by them, heard by them, to be understood and touched by them.

—Virginia Satir

Around this time Cindy got engaged and threw herself into planning her upcoming wedding. We were still having rehearsals with our new director and performing in clubs all over Manhattan. As Cindy was so busy with the wedding, I started spending more time with another woman in the group named Cynthia (aka Cindy 3.5?). While socializing we began making a lot of executive decisions about the comedy group. We planned a rehearsal to cover some of the finer points of a show that was coming up. I knew how busy Cindy was, and that she didn't really need to be at the rehearsal, so I didn't tell her about it—HUGE, OVERLY ASSUMPTIVE, CODE-PENDENT MISTAKE.

When we all got together with the director for the final run-through before the show, Cindy, of course, had heard about the rehearsal she hadn't been told about and was angry. During the rehearsal she began making sarcastic cracks at me whenever I spoke, which made me angry, and I would snipe back. Within a very short time it turned into a take-no-prisoners bloodbath. The director, a very wise woman, declared the rehearsal over, sent the other women home and told Cindy and me that we were going to stay and clean up this mess.

The three of us settled in on the sofa. With no other bodies in the way we really hunkered down to have what I thought would be a to-the-death fight. The director said, "How did this all start?" Cindy jumped in right away with, "Kathy planned a rehearsal and didn't even tell me about it." I shot back, "It wasn't an important rehearsal and you didn't even need to be there." Cindy spat out, "I'm just as important in this group as you are and I should have been told about it." Revving up to a full head of self-righteous fury, I snarked out,

"You're busy planning your wedding and I was trying to free you up so you had some extra time." That's when the miracle happened.

Cindy says now, in hindsight, that she realized in that moment how important our relationship was and she didn't want to lose it. Remember, up till this point we had been having an easy, breezy friendship. We socialized, worked, starved and performed together but the friendship had never really been put to the test. At this point she did something in the argument that no one had ever done with me before—she was completely honest about her feelings, even though she was afraid it would make her sound foolish. She said, "You've been spending so much time with Cynthia that I was feeling left out." Her calm honesty stripped me of all my anger and I said, "You're so busy getting married that I didn't feel you had time for me, and I started hanging around with Cynthia because she's fun and knows a lot of straight guys." We started to laugh and, as always with honesty and laughter, there I was healing.

CROWN JEWEL

Shared joy is double joy.
Shared sorrow is half sorrow.
—Swedish Proverb

Our friend and coworker at WCBS-TV, Bill Sherwood, wrote a part for me in his movie *Parting Glances*. After it opened I was offered a job on a film in Los Angeles, so I went there to work for two weeks. Twenty-four years later I still live here. I made a lot of new friends and even a good one that I found out later had been named Cindy at birth but had hated the name and so changed it to something more stylish. In the end I lost touch with all of the other Cindys. Life and distance have a way of doing that.

On one of my trips back to Wisconsin to visit my mother, I looked up the First Cindy, who by now was married and had children. I hadn't seen her in years, and yet the minute we were together I could feel the unconditional love and comfort I had always felt with her when we were children. During that visit we reconnected and both realized exactly how important we are to each other. It was a great gift to be given back that friendship. We now enjoy the immeasurable satisfaction of knowing that we will always be there for one another. We e-mail and call often just to remind each other that someone somewhere loves us, and sometimes to simply say hi.

I've been in a long-term relationship with a man who hates to travel. It has always been a sore point between us because I so dearly love it. I wanted to take a vacation and go to Paris. I hadn't spoken to the Third Cindy in a few months but out of the blue I had the impulse to ask her if she wanted to go with me (I now like to think it was my Queen voice—the one that tells me to run, play, smile and, in this case, have fun with Cindy Ratzlaff).

The only way to have a friend is to be one.
—Ralph Waldo Emerson

We had a great time on that first trip to Paris. We walked, ate, talked, shopped, people-watched and talked some more. After that, whenever I wanted to take a trip I would first ask my boyfriend if he wanted to go, and when he said no I would call Cindy and she would say yes. We took some wonderful vacations and during those trips we regained and strengthened our friendship—the easy, breezy part and the honest and true part.

My epic tale of Cindys found, Cindys lost and Cindys regained fills me with wonder. I have a small trusted inner circle of Ladies-in-Waiting who want nothing more for me than my happiness. I bring with me, to this circle, qualities that I learned in my friendship with the First Cindy and that I am reminded of daily in my friendship with Cindy Ratzlaff—love, honesty, generosity and bravery. Not all of my LIW are named Cindy but I am grateful for the abundance of brilliant, beloved Cindys that I have known.

Of course, there are slips and slides along the way but I believe that we are trying, to the best of our ability, to be good and decent friends to one another. By surrounding myself with this strong circle of noble women, I have the courage to take risks in my life. My agenda-free LIW make me feel safe in the knowledge that whether I fail or succeed, I will still have their unconditional love and respect. What more could a Queen ask for?

• • •

Your inner circle is just that—a circle. You have a responsibility to be the kind of friend you want to have. It's great to have trusted LIW to help you process your problems and issues. A good thing to keep in mind is that there's a very fine line between processing and whining. Everybody steps in the pity puddle once in a while but it's hard to support someone who is constantly living in the problem and not looking for a solution. A couple of our fellow Queens, when the whining becomes excessive, tell each other to "Queen Up!" We love that phrase and we think it's good advice—sometimes you just have to let go of the details, move forward and Queen Up!

WHAT WE DID TO CREATE DEEP, FULFILLING FRIENDSHIPS AND BUILD OUR COURTS

First, we've learned in our more than thirty years of friendship that you get what you give. We offer each other a safe place to be ourselves based on a history of nonjudgment and unconditional love. In a friendship, when you have the courage to be yourself and be vulnerable, it creates a safe place for everyone to be themselves. This is true for old friends and new acquaintances, no matter where you meet.

Cindy took a series of "webinars" online. She was meeting other students in the members-only Web site where they chatted about the classwork and asked one another questions. The final classes were to be held in person in San Diego and everyone was in charge of making their own travel arrangements. One of the women Cindy had been chatting with posted on the site, asking if anyone wanted to room with her. Cindy responded that she would love to. In return, by way of introduction she got this charming e-mail:

Hi, Cindy,

I realize that we don't know each other well so I thought I would write a little "roomie bio" so you know what you're getting into. LOL…

★   I am a morning person and try to make it to the gym…I have way too much energy.

★   I start the day with a protein shake…promise to only power shake it for one min.

★   My two favorite girls when traveling are my laptop and iPhone so I'm never traveling alone.

★   I don't hog the bathroom…I need little time to get ready.

★   I don't smoke but love wine…a girl has to have her vices.

★   I love to shop for shoes and bags…okay, another set of vices.

★   If I'm very tired, I tend to snore a little bit so carry earplugs for sensitive roomies.

★   I have two little divas-in-training that I will miss very much since by the time we meet I'll have been gone from home nine days.

★   Most of all, I LOVE to have FUN! So I hope you're in for lots of it!

Have a great Tuesday,

Lisa ♥

Lisa was so honest and open about who she was that Cindy was instantly put at ease and responded like this:

> Dear Lisa,
>
> I love this!! Okay, here's mine.
>
> I am a morning person. I tend to wake up very early...like 5:30 or 6:00 a.m. I usually head out immediately in search of coffee—I need to drink coffee and read the paper to get going. Oh, how I wish I was a gym person... maybe you'll inspire me.
>
> ★ I love red wine...and white wine....
>
> ★ I don't think I snore but I can't guarantee it. My hubby does so I'm really good at sleeping with earplugs.
>
> ★ I have a secret handbag jones so my business better start taking off because Mama needs a new one soon.
>
> ★ My daughter just finished her first year of college and I'll miss her and her dad while we're in San Diego but I'm looking forward to this so much.
>
> ★ I hate to drive when I'm in unfamiliar territory so I'm hoping someone else loves to drive, and I'd be happy to chip in on car costs or cab rides.
>
> ★ I can't wait. This should be a ball.
>
> All best,
>
> Cindy

Lisa had the courage to be herself in her e-mail and Cindy responded in kind. They are well on their way to being good friends and they haven't even met. It's possible to find new LIW anywhere if you are willing to be open and honest and to be yourself.

Secondly, we believe the basis of our friendship and of all our friendships is the four virtues we chose to define our Queen: loving, honest, generous and brave. These are our core values—who we really are. We seek to surround ourselves with like-minded women who share our core values. The reason this is so necessary is that these women reflect back to us the attributes that are most important to us. These friendships nurture and enhance those qualities, making them shine and bringing out the best in us.

Finally, we show up. We work at being good friends to one another. We practice active listening and we give one another the gift of time. For us, in making sure that we are a good friend to someone who is a good friend to us, we become better women. And we want that for you.

HERE'S WHAT YOU CAN DO

First, we need to take a look at the support system you have in place. Take a piece of paper and, down the left-hand side, write the names of the women you consider to be your closest friends. Now, across the top of the paper, write the four virtues you chose in Chapter 4 to define your Queen. Next to your friends' names put a check for each of the virtues you think they have.

LIW	QUALITIES OF YOUR QUEEN			
	LOVING	HONEST	GENEROUS	BRAVE
Doris	✓			
Cynthia	✓	✓	✓	✓
Hester Sue		✓		
First Cindy	✓	✓	✓	✓

Do you have a friend who has a check in all the categories? Do you have two? If you find yourself with friends who have checks in all the columns, these are your true inner circle, your LIW. It's time to tell them. There is enormous power in acknowledging someone's positive effect in your life. Don't be afraid to be completely honest and show your true feelings. Write a note, e-mail or make a phone call to each woman on your list who you've determined is part of your inner circle. You can elaborate as much or as little as you want about what they mean to you and how much you value their friendship. If you're not comfortable going into detail, you can simply tell them you're glad they're in your life and leave it at that. We think you'll be surprised to find how your friendships will grow even stronger when you have the courage to name them out loud.

CROWN JEWEL

Appreciation can make a day, even change a life. Your willingness to put it into words is all that is necessary.

—Margaret Cousins

Perhaps you find yourself, at this time in your life with friends who have very few checkmarks or possibly with no close friends at all. Don't despair. It happens to us all at one time or another in life. The good news is that just as quickly as we think we have no candidates for LIW, one will appear. Look around you during your day. Is there a woman who crosses your path at work, the gym, church, yoga class or your favorite bistro who you enjoy talking to or admire? Find an interesting movie or event and ask her if she'd like to go with you. The worst thing that could happen is she might say no, but there's a good chance that she's in the market for an LIW, as well.

Remember how easy it was when you were nine and all you had to do was ask someone if they wanted to be your friend? It's still an option. We have a fellow Queen named Susan who realized that she didn't have any friends who were her age and felt a longing to have one. There was a woman in a class she was taking that she enjoyed talking to and so one day she took a deep breath and sincerely said, "I'm looking for a friend who's my age. Would you like to be my friend?" The woman replied, "I would love to be your friend." They have been friends ever since and have, for many years now, been trusted LIW in each other's lives.

It can be that simple. Just take a deep breath and ask someone you admire if they will be your friend. The point is to keep trying, because your courage may be rewarded with an addition to your inner circle. The world is packed full of wonderful women that are all potential LIW. If you make building your court and nurturing these vital relationships the cornerstone of the second half of your life, then you will truly be a remarkable Queen.

ROYAL PROCLAMATION

From this moment forward I will surround myself with loving, honest, brave, generous and agenda-free LIW, understanding that, in order to have great friends, I must be a great friend. It's what the Queen wants, what the Queen needs and what the Queen deserves. Long live the Queen!

CHAPTER 6

honesty [ŏn-ĭ-stē] (noun) 1. the quality or condition of being honest 2. truthfulness 3. sincerity 4. frankness or candor 5. openness 6. integrity 7. genuineness 8. virtue 9. freedom from deceit and fraud

ESTABLISH FIRM BOUNDARIES THAT WILL STRENGTHEN ALL YOUR RELATIONSHIPS

. . . or . . .

The Huns Are at the Border

With a court of trusted Ladies-In-Waiting by your side, helping you reign, you are strong beyond belief. Please be sure and let them know how valuable they are to you, because you're really going to need their help soon—like right now. Danger is lurking much closer than you realize—the Huns are gathering at your border.

As we travel the country talking to groups of women, what we hear most often is, "I'd like to banish my entire family because they're sucking the very life out of me." This is always followed by wild hoots of agreeing laughter. The truth is that banishing your family is not the answer—they very well may be sucking the joy out of your life, but if they are it's because you're letting them. It's time to give yourself the gift of establishing clear, firm boundaries. We promise you this will be one of the best gifts you ever give yourself.

Setting strong boundaries is an essential skill for a Queen. Without them everyone—your family, friends, neighbors and even the mailman—will be able to drain your energy. We call the people who breach your territory the Huns. They are already massed on your borders. Some Huns will take advantage of you accidentally and others will do it on purpose. However, it's not their fault.

CROWN JEWEL

Be who you are and say what you feel, because those who mind don't matter and those who matter don't mind.

—Dr. Seuss

The Huns are just neighboring tribes who don't really understand territorial boundaries. They're nomads. They will wander onto your turf with their sheep and, if you allow them, will let the fluffy critters devour all of your grass and drink their fill of your water. They don't always mean any harm, although some of them do. Most Huns are simply trying to take care of themselves and can be persuaded to follow the rules and respect your boundaries if you're clear about where and what those boundaries are. None of them could wreak any kind of havoc if you weren't standing on your own border, holding the gate wide open, with a big sign that says Enter Here—All Huns Welcome!

We have all experienced the uncomfortable feeling of doing something that we don't want to do or don't have time to do because we said yes when we really, really desperately wanted to say no. Have you ever promised to deliver baked goods to a charity function on a day when you had two doctors' appointments and a business lunch? Ever just answered the phone and suddenly discovered you're hosting twenty-three people for the holidays and one is a vegan and three are gluten intolerant and your original meal plan was whole-wheat lasagna? Do you still wonder exactly when you agreed to keep the neighbors' dog while they toured Europe, which has forced you to bring in a pet sitter yourself because you have a business trip?

⋯⋯⋯⋯⋯⋯ CROWN JEWEL ⋯⋯⋯⋯⋯⋯

**The truth is always exciting.
Speak it, then. Life is dull without it.**
—Pearl S. Buck

Remember Bette Davis in the classic movie *Now, Voyager?* She plays Charlotte Vale, the youngest daughter of an old-moneyed Boston family. As a girl Charlotte is pretty and shows

a bit of spunk when her controlling mother attempts to domi-
nate her. But as she grows older, Charlotte becomes more and
more afraid of her mother's disapproval and so always ends up
giving in and saying yes when she desperately wants to scream
no. Within a few years she is overweight, her eyebrows have
pulled a Frieda Kahlo and she ends up in a mental hospital,
twitching with unhappiness and resentment. Of course, because it's a movie, Charlotte learns to set boundaries in the
hospital; she slims down, gets a new wardrobe and a complete
makeover (including the eyebrows) and ends up on a cruise,
wearing an awesome hat. It wouldn't have made for much of
a movie but it would have been grand if Charlotte could have
just learned to say no before she gained the weight and got
hauled off to the locked ward.

The truth is that a lot of women have difficulty setting clear
boundaries and so they say yes, mean no and become resentful.
This isn't good for you or fair to those around you. When you
say yes, people have every right to believe that you mean yes.
When you say no, you have the right to have that no respected.
Boundary crossing happens at work and at home. For some it
only occurs with a certain Hun but for others they simply can't
say no to anyhun (sorry about the pun).

There are many reasons why we say yes instead of no. Most
commonly we hear women talk about wanting to be liked,
needing to please others and being afraid to disappoint people
if they say no. Then there are the official martyrs who say yes
because they believe they are the only ones who can or will

do it right. In the end the reason doesn't really matter. All you need to know is the key to setting a strong boundary starts with you.

Your inability to say what you mean and mean what you say is the issue. The solution is recognizing your limits and needs, then making the choice to take care of yourself by setting clear, firm boundaries. And doing it all in the kind of supportive language that leaves no casualties behind—including yourself.

CINDY

I have two younger sisters and a brother. We are all very different in looks, attitudes toward life and opinions on just about everything from politics to how to raise children. What we do share, though, is the official Ratzlaff crest—a suit of armor tightly wrapped with clinging vines and our family motto above it: Personal Boundaries Are Meant to Be Crossed!

My sisters and I grew up borrowing one another's clothes and sharing a bedroom, a bathroom, a car and, at times, boyfriends. It was no different for our brother. As soon as he was born he was pulled into the vortex of our overlapping lives. The only difference was he didn't borrow our clothes.

Our lives were so closely intertwined that sometimes you couldn't tell who was inhaling and who was exhaling. This boundaryless relationship of our childhood has followed us into adulthood. Mostly, it's a loving experience and we value our closeness. Mostly. Sometimes the daily phone calls we make to stay in touch turn into meddling, manipulating and inappropriate requests. On the occasions when this happens we suddenly go from being family members to being card-carrying Huns at one another's borders.

After nearly three decades in the business world I have learned how to set firm workplace boundaries, to be very clear with people about projects, deadlines, goals and budgets. If appropriate, I can say no to people in a business setting faster than you can blink an eye. But, for me, setting firm boundaries and saying no to family and friends has been a difficult lesson to learn.

CROWN JEWEL

**Life shrinks or expands
in proportion to one's courage.**

—Anaïs Nin

In business I've developed a way to safeguard my borders with my good friend Mary, who acts as my Vice President of Tone Check. Whenever I need to send some tricky correspondence or have a difficult discussion with a client or colleague, I write a draft of what I want to send or say. I call Mary for a "tone check" and she reads my draft and gives me feedback. She'll tell me, from an objective point of view, whether or not I've conveyed my message clearly or if I'm completely off the mark. She helps me figure out if I've left any point unspoken so that I can achieve my goal of being clear. She also helps me take the excess emotion out of the communication and warns me if I've gone from Queen to Drama Queen.

Here's a personal example of why this tool comes in so handy. The other day at 5:00 a.m., way before the crack of dawn, I was sitting in my flannel pajamas and white fuzzy slippers, drinking my first cup of coffee and reading my e-mails. I opened an e-mail from a client that really ticked me off. I didn't like her tone and I felt underappreciated. I shot off a snippy reply, reminding her of everything I'd done to date and calling into question her tone in the e-mail. The instant I pressed Send, I thought, *Oh, crap.*

As Mary later pointed out to me, it's easy to misinterpret e-mails at any time of the day but early morning, before the caffeine kicks in, is especially hazardous. Well, to make a long and embarrassing story short, I talked it over with Mary, and after reading the client's e-mail, she pointed out that the tone seemed more abrupt than abusive. She said that I had probably misunderstood the point, overreacted and most likely owed the client an apology.

It was hard to hear what Mary had to say because I'm not usually one to fly off the handle. I am generally the logical, rational person who helps calm and motivate everyone else. As Mary is one of my trusted LIW, I knew her read on the situation was true. Also, the truly icky feeling that flooded my body when I pressed Send was a very loud warning bell. I'm human and I made a mistake. I'd let an early-morning lack of caffeine call me into a battle that didn't even exist.

I immediately wrote a draft e-mail to my client, apologizing for my inappropriately sharp response and offered to speak to her by phone so we could get to the bottom of our misunderstanding. I ran this draft by Mary *before* pressing Send (how smart would it have been to do this the first time?). My courage and honesty paid off. My client and I had a great exchange, cleared the air and have continued working together with new respect for each other.

With much success using my VP of Tone Check to help me set boundaries in my business life, I've adapted this tool in my personal life. Kathy is the Lady-in-Waiting I most often go to for help in setting those personal boundaries. Just as I do with Mary, I call Kathy to talk over a particular Hun-based issue— almost always a situation where I want to say no, but I think I must say yes. We talk it through, and I come to a decision about what I need and what I want to do. As I practice what I want to say, Kathy will give me the thumbs-up or asks me to be clearer or less self-righteous or to tone down the anger. Then I just do it. After I have that conversation, I call Kathy back and we talk about how it went and think about whether any additional work needs to be done to set the boundary or clean up the communication. We call this "bookending."

Sometimes it's easy to reclaim my boundary from the Huns and sometimes it's just plain messy. At first it felt uncomfortable saying no, but the more I do it the easier it gets. And I'm willing to put in the work because I'm already feeling the results. My relationship with my family has grown stronger as I practice setting limits. There is no unspoken resentment. Now when I say yes, my family is assured that I really want to do what I've agreed to do. I've realized that by learning to say no, my yes has become more valuable.

• • •

Being a good Queen means being able to speak up for yourself. That includes telling another person the truth about a request or behavior not being acceptable, and saying it in such clear, supportive language that it doesn't damage the relationship. This can be a very tricky thing to learn because there are so many emotional issues tied up in putting our own needs and ourselves first.

There is a strong myth that being a good caretaker, spouse, friend and neighbor means you must say yes. So many women have the fear that if someone asks something of them and they say no, they will be considered to be selfish or thoughtless or found to be unlikeable. Consider this, however. Have you ever asked a friend or family member to help you with something? You would feel terrible if they said yes and then resented you because they really wanted to say no. You assume that if they didn't want to or couldn't help you they would tell you. You owe them the same.

This is such an important gift that it's worth the sometimes uncomfortable practice that it will take to learn the skill. Mastering it will set you free and protect your friends and family from the effects of resentment, which can undermine your relationships.

KATHY

My parents raised me on a need-to-know basis. When I was four they said, "Get in the car." I said, "Where are we going?" They said, "The hospital." I said, "Why?" They said, "You're getting your tonsils out." I always felt they underestimated the amount of information I needed to get by. Anyway, later that day, when I woke up in the recovery room in pain and minus my tonsils, I had my first nun sighting. To me these women seemed very serious and a bit frightening. They were from the local convent—the Sisters of the Sorrowful Mother. The town was predominantly Polish Catholic and the hospital was a Catholic hospital. Unfortunately for me, my family was neither Polish nor Catholic.

I was sharing a hospital room with another little girl around my age who had also had her tonsils removed. She told me that the nuns were nice and would get me whatever I wanted, including ice cream. At that moment a nun came in and indeed asked her if she needed anything. The nun suggested a back rub and began lovingly to smooth some lotion on the girl's back.

My throat really hurt. Reassured by the little girl's testimony and the sister's obvious kindness, I told the nun that my throat was really sore and asked if I could please have some ice cream. At first she ignored me, but when she finished the back rub, she came over to my bed and just stared at me, then walked out the door. I had never seen it before in real life—only on TV—but that nun looked at me with eyes full of hate. I was shocked and terrified. Needless to say, I never got any ice cream, or a back rub or for that matter, even a smile.

No one had ever been mean to me before. I had no idea what I had done wrong. I assumed there was something not right with me. Otherwise, why would the nuns stare at me with such hatred? For the rest of the time in the hospital I was very quiet and never asked for anything. I was frightened and I was four, so this strategy made perfect sense to me.

This is not a story about Catholics versus Methodists and I don't hate nuns. I'm just saying it's the first experience I remember where I should have spoken up for myself or at least told my parents what was going on so that they could speak for me but I didn't. In fact, I never told my parents what happened, because I was sure it was my fault that the nuns hated me and I was ashamed.

I internalized everything and became a very stoic child. The summer before I turned six, I was watching the neighbor girl wash her dog in the backyard. I was barefoot and stepped on a piece of wood with a nail sticking out of it. The nail pierced my foot and all I said was, "I have to go home now." Later, when my mom asked the neighbor girl what had happened, she had no idea, because when I'd stepped on the nail my expression hadn't even changed. I was on the path to being a great poker player.

I'm not going to bore you with all of my "Kathy was a weird child and an odd adult" stories, although I have a bunch of them. I just couldn't speak up for myself. If I was at a viola lesson and my nose started to run, I was too ashamed to stop and ask for a tissue, so I would sniff through the whole lesson. After I got older, I had jobs that were horrible but I was too embarrassed to quit. Instead, I would have Cindy call and pretend to be my cousin, saying that my mother had died and I wouldn't be coming back. I didn't want to disappoint anyone, so I took what I thought was the easy way out.

I wanted everyone to like me, and I thought if I said yes everyone would. It was as if *no* was not even in my vocabulary. I realize now I never spoke up for myself because my self-esteem was below sea level. I would smile and pretend to be pleasant, nodding and saying yes, but underneath I was always seething with resentment. I felt angry at everybody for trying to take advantage of me. It never occurred to me that the problem was me. I lived for years like a ticking time bomb headed for one heck of a big bang.

CROWN JEWEL

Be yourself; everyone else is already taken.
—Oscar Wilde

I moved to New York and really enjoyed living in Manhattan. I'd had several more horrible jobs during the first few years that Cindy had "helped me quit" but now I was supporting myself by doing secretarial work. I was performing improvisational comedy regularly in clubs and this led to a few small acting parts. I still wasn't any good at setting boundaries or speaking up for myself, but I had created a life where few people challenged me and I could just sort of fly under the radar.

I took a vacation and went to Los Angeles for a week to go to the opening of the movie I had done—*Parting Glances*. While I was in Los Angeles, there was a small murder-arson incident in my building back in New York and the resulting fire burned most of the apartment building. While many of the apartments suffered severe fire and water damage, mine was untouched. So when I got home from my vacation, I continued to live there.

Living in a burned-out building in midtown Manhattan can be a bit stressful. The few of us that were left in the building had to work very hard to keep it safe and running smoothly. The landlord had stopped providing all services, hoping the rest of us would move out and he could turn the building into luxury condos. The walls in the hallways were burned and peeling. The odor of damp, charred wood permeated everything. There were rats, pimps and crack whores roaming the halls every night. Living in my apartment was like being in the middle of a war zone but the good news was that I had a two-bedroom apartment with an eat-in kitchen in midtown Manhattan for free. Yippee! Somebody with a little more self-esteem might have moved out. Not me—I lived there for three more years.

With the money I was saving on rent, I finally decided to go back to Los Angeles for a well-needed vacation. I stayed with a couple of old friends, who very graciously let me sleep up in the loft area of their condo on one of those little foldout foam sofas. One morning five months later, I woke up and realized something my friends had known for a long time—I wasn't just visiting anymore...I was living there.

As an actor in Los Angeles I needed all the basics—home, job, friends, car and agent. I started by accidentally getting an agent. One morning, while staying with my friends, I was sitting in my pajamas, having breakfast, after they had left for work when their neighbor stopped by for coffee. I invited him in, and while I ate my cereal I chattered away about my life in the burned-out building. When my friends came home from work that night, they told me their neighbor was an agent and he wanted to represent me. For someone as shy as I was, meeting an agent while in my pj's, eating cereal, was probably the only way I could have gotten one.

My agent began sending me out for character roles he thought I was right for. I called them "the four Ns"—Nannies, Nuns, Nurses and Nazis. Visually I was right for the parts but I never got the roles because I was too insecure to assert myself. The truth is, it's hard to act like a grouchy nun or cranky nanny if speaking up for yourself is a problem. I would work on each role carefully, but when I got into the audition I couldn't get it right. I always came across as too vulnerable—which, for example, is not something they were usually looking for in a Nazi.

As the years passed I did manage to get cast in a few odd acting roles in movies and TV but I was mostly supporting myself by working out of an agency as a temporary secretary. I might have gone on forever not speaking up for myself if it weren't for a potent cocktail of misinformation and rudeness.

My agent sent me to a last-minute audition to replace someone on a television pilot that was currently being shot. He told me to pick up the script when I got there. He didn't have much information about the role, so I put on my faux Armani suit, and thinking I looked the best I could, I headed out. And now the true story of how I got cast as Mimi on *The Drew Carey Show.*

When I got to the audition, the room was filled with actresses that had on wacky clothes and big, wild, weird hairdos. That's when I realized either my agent or I had missed some vital piece of information. That vital bit of information was printed on the top of the script they handed me. As I mentioned before, the character description was "this woman is completely visually wrong to sell cosmetics and is the meanest, ugliest woman in the world." Oops. Compared to everyone else, I was dressed very conservatively. All I could hope for was that it would help me stand out.

I quickly read over the lines and tried to build up some oomph to put behind the mean part but, as I said, I wasn't good at mean. I did not have high expectations for getting the job. When they called me into the room for the audition, there sat a director that I had worked with a few times. On set he had a terrible temper and an abusive personality. Someone told me that he had been a Broadway director and felt that TV was beneath him and that was why he was angry all the time. All I knew was when he worked, he was smart enough to not pick on the regulars and only took his anger out on the new person, and I had always been the new person.

That day he was in a truly evil mood—it was coming off him in waves. I suppose it was because they were in the middle of shooting the pilot and had to stop to replace someone that wasn't working out. As I took my seat he announced to the room, "Oh, here she is. She thinks she's so f***ing funny." I felt as if I had been slapped hard across the face. Everyone else in the room looked at the floor until finally the casting director said, "I'll be reading with you. Shall we get started?" As he began to run the scene with me I think I was in a bit of shock from the director's rudeness. Suddenly, right in the middle of the audition, the director yelled for me to stop. He said, "Kathy, Kathy, Kathy, what the f**k are you doing? This woman is angry, all right? She's angry—can you do that? Can you? Just try it again."

It's curious what brings about that moment when you can no longer be silent and your voice is released. It happened for me in that instant. I was so angry I couldn't even see straight. I launched back into that scene with a barely contained fury that flung me up out of my chair and right into the face of the startled casting director. As I was coming to the end of the scene I walked to the door, flung it open, turned and literally spat out the last line back into the room, then slammed the door behind me with all my might and went home.

CROWN JEWEL

**Only when we are no longer afraid
do we begin to live.**

—Dorothy Thompson

I got the job, and what was just supposed to be a week of work turned into nine years of playing Mimi on *The Drew Carey Show*. I told you how playing the meanest, ugliest woman in the world miraculously and ironically helped me claim my beauty. The truth is that the miracle was twofold. The second part was the amazing osmosis that happened as I began to take in Mimi's abrasive determination and guts and she began to absorb my vulnerability and low self-esteem.

It became easier and easier to take care of myself with Mimi by my side. And I needed help because I was now surrounded by hundreds of Huns daily. With her rudeness tempered by my shyness I was able to say no, set boundaries, keep all the Huns at bay and do it all without pain to myself or a large body count. If a situation occurred where my borders were in immediate danger and I became stuck, I would simply ask myself, "What would Mimi say?" Then I'd add the love and set the boundary.

Mimi really knew how to take care of herself. She could set

a boundary that a squadron of tanks with air support couldn't break through. Of course, she wasn't very good at supportive language but, then again, she was just a character on TV. Yet, she taught me a lot and I still rely on what I learned from her. So, I'm offering you one of the greatest gifts I've ever been given...Mimi. The next time your boundaries are about to be assaulted by a Hun and you don't know what to do, just ask yourself, "What would Mimi say?" Then add the love and set the boundary.

• • •

Every realm needs boundaries. If it weren't for those borders, hostile forces could invade your territory, lay siege to your castle and pillage your most valued possession (*your* peace of mind). When the Queen is very clear about boundaries, she actually does a service to all concerned. We think the airline industry really has the right idea on boundary setting. As you prepare for takeoff, the flight attendant launches into her safety spiel that usually ends with, "In the event of a loss of cabin pressure, the oxygen masks will drop down. Please put your own mask on before attempting to help those around you." Makes sense, doesn't it? If you're gasping for air and near to blacking out, you're absolutely useless to those around you who might need assistance. But if you take care of yourself, keeping the oxygen flowing, you'll be able to reach over and help the person next to you with their mask. Then you'll both be able to breathe.

CROWN JEWEL

> **Life is either a daring adventure or nothing. Security is mostly a superstition. It does not exist in nature.**
>
> —Helen Keller

We know a Queen who three times a year says no to family and friends and takes herself off on a retreat. It's definitely a much-needed rest for her but it also ends up being a gift for everyone around her. She returns to her life refreshed, restored and better able to be a patient mother and a supportive friend. Think of it this way: if you do what's best for you, then you do what's best for everybody.

Learning to set your boundaries right away will help you become almost invincible to invasions from the Huns. It's much harder and messier to establish your borders when they have already been crossed (think *Thelma and Louise*). Wouldn't it be great if you could be honest and say what you mean right away with no acting out, no pent-up explosion and then just move on? You can do it by mastering this skill and then practicing it. If you do, we promise you'll feel more in control of your life, happier helping others and significantly less overwhelmed and resentful.

WHAT WE DID TO ESTABLISH FIRM BOUNDARIES AND STRENGTHEN OUR RELATIONSHIPS

As women who used to say yes when we wanted to say no, we added a new phrase to our vocabularies. Whenever anyone asks us for something, we say, "Hmm, let me think about that and get back to you." It buys us time to have a private conversation with ourselves about whether or not we can or want to do what we've been asked. We found that taking that moment brings clarity and allows us to give an honest answer.

During our Crowning Ceremony, when we finally came to the realization that we needed to strengthen our boundaries and post notice to the Huns, we decided to tackle this task together. In thinking about the people we harbored the most resentment against, we were able to identify our biggest Huns. It became clear to us just how much emotional energy and anxiety we had been expending on them. We decided that here, at the beginning of the second half of our lives, we would confront this nonsense once and for all. We would Queen Up!

We each identified one particular Hun-based border crossing that was making us feel stress and decided to tackle the issue head-on. We found it helped us to think about these Huns as friendly nomads who didn't necessarily understand or recognize borders. So it was our job to clearly point them out and then guard them.

Using our bookending tool, we called each other, stated who the Hun was and discussed what we wanted to say in our boundary-setting speech. When we were certain that we could be clear without being angry, we made a phone call to our Hun. In the call we lovingly took responsibility for our part in the border dispute, which was that we never let the Hun know that there was even a border to be crossed in the first place. We set the new boundary, thanked the Hun for listening and closed the conversation. Then we called each other to talk it over, recap what had been said and get advice on whether or not we had resolved the issue and whether there was any lingering resentment that needed our attention.

Now whatever combination we use of "What would Mimi do, then add the love" or "Hmm, I'll get back to you" or bookending, we're covered. We call on these tools whenever a Hun ventures too near our borders, which seems to be less and less now that they are clearly marked. We are now the Queens who might say yes or no but who always mean what they say.

CROWN JEWEL

I'm not afraid of storms,
for I'm learning to sail my ship.
—Louisa May Alcott

HERE'S WHAT YOU CAN DO

We've created a battle plan to help you repel the Huns.

Why

are you snapping at loved ones,
feeling low-grade anxiety, using your caller
ID to screen your calls, drinking an extra
glass of wine at night or reaching for
the candy dish (think Bette Davis in the
party scene of *All About Eve*)?
A Hun has crossed your border.

Who

is really causing you stress? Instead of tormenting
yourself and innocent others, identify the real
Hun. Choose one Hun at a time.

What

boundary have you allowed to be crossed?

Clean It Up

a. Call one of your trusted LIW and use her as a sounding board to practice your boundary-setting speech. She will help you find supportive language (remember the goal is no casualties).

b. Decide where you are going to confront the Hun. Meeting in person is a good choice if the Hun is family or a close friend because the tool of hugging may be used. The telephone also works well because you can get in, say your piece and get out easily. You could e-mail but this is not usually recommended, because you can't control the Hun's perception of your written word.

c. Then just do it. Remember, what would Mimi say, then add the love.

d. Bookend it. When you're done setting the boundary, call your LIW back to talk over what just happened. You want to check to see if any more cleaning up is necessary or if there is closure and the Hun is safely back on their side of the border.

Repeat

steps 1 through 4 until all the Huns are repelled and you are calm and breathing easy.

Keep in mind our LIW and families are not mind readers. As the Queen, you have to let them know what your boundaries are. Being honest and setting strong borders will protect you and those around you. If you are clear about your personal boundaries—what you will or will not do—your friends and family will learn to respect and honor you and your choices. Setting firm boundaries will strengthen your alliances and friendships and ultimately allow you to be happier in all your relationships. And a happy Queen is, well, just that, a happy Queen.

ROYAL PROCLAMATION

I decree from this day forth, I will embrace
the power of "no." I will mean what I say
and say what I mean.

When confronted by a Hun at my border,
I will not be afraid. I will ask myself,
"What would Mimi say?" Then I'll add
the love and set my boundary.

I Queen Up well.

CHAPTER 7

happy [ha-pē] (adjective) 1. contented 2. glad
3. joyful 4. satisfied 5. blissful 6. feeling pleasure
7. blessed 8. delighted 9. relieved
10. on cloud nine

DISCOVER THE SIMPLE TRICK TO FINALLY BEING HAPPY

. . . or . . .

It's Time to Poop or Get Off the Pot

Well done. You've put your battle plan into effect and have brought peace to your borderlands and the Huns. We imagine right about now you're wondering, "Aren't I ready to be Queen YET?? When do I get to wear the crown?" The answer is soon, very soon. There's just one more gift you need to give yourself before you're truly ready to be Queen—making the choice to be happy.

As it turns out being happy isn't something you're born knowing how to do, like breathing or blinking. It's a skill you have to learn and practice, such as riding a bike. But once you know how to be happy, just like with riding a bike, you'll never forget how to do it and the results will be fun and effortless.

CROWN JEWEL

**Happiness is not a station you arrive at,
but a manner of traveling.**
—Margaret Lee Runbeck

Do you live your life contented or do you still think there are some things you need before you can be happy? Be honest. Have you fallen into the I'll-be-happy-when trap? "I'll be happy when I'm thinner," "I'll be happy when I have more money," or "I'll be happy when I'm in the perfect relationship." What if none of those things ever happen? Does that mean you can never be happy? Is putting off being happy how you want to live the second half of your life?

Have you ever heard the old adage "Yesterday is history, tomorrow a mystery, today is a gift. That's why it's called the present"? When you're always living for the future, it's impossible to enjoy life today. The truth is that you have everything you need right now to be happy, and it's finally time to acknowledge that and grasp it at the deepest level of your being.

If you've been telling yourself that there are just a few more things you need before you can claim happiness, then this is the moment to stop telling yourself tall tales and wasting your valuable time. Think what you could do with all the energy you squandered away worrying about what you don't have.

CROWN JEWEL

Happiness is a choice that requires effort at times.

—Anonymous

There's an old Midwestern saying that we've cleaned up a bit but definitely applies here: "It's time to poop or get off the pot" about being happy.

Remember the charming old book by Eleanor H. Porter called *Pollyanna*? It's the story of a young girl who is orphaned and must go live in Vermont with her strict Aunt Polly. Very wealthy but unhappy, aunt Polly rules the town with an iron fist, making it a very unpleasant place to live.

Pollyanna lives her life by playing the "Glad Game," a positive way of looking at life. The game is about finding something to be glad about in every situation. For instance, her aunt makes her sleep in the dusty, hot attic but Pollyanna is glad that she has a small window with a beautiful view. When Pollyanna is late for dinner her aunt punishes her by sending her to the kitchen to eat only bread and milk. Pollyanna is glad because she really likes bread (who doesn't?) and she likes spending time with Nancy, who works in the kitchen.

With her upbeat attitude toward life, Pollyanna slowly changes the unhappy town into a pleasant place to live and

shows the townspeople, by example, how to find the joy in life.
When Pollyanna is hurt in a car accident and loses the use of
her legs she becomes depressed and is no longer able to be glad.
The people of the town come and visit, letting her know how
much her optimistic attitude has touched their lives. Pollyanna
regains her glad attitude and her ability to walk.

CROWN JEWEL

> **Let us rise up and be thankful,
> for if we didn't learn a lot today, at least
> we learned a little, and if we didn't learn
> a little, at least we didn't get sick, and if
> we got sick, at least we didn't die;
> so, let us all be thankful.**
>
> —Buddha

We could all take a lesson from Pollyanna about finding the
positive in every moment and letting go of our fear and unhappiness. Dwelling in the negative aspects of your life will keep
you from seeing all the gifts that are around you. Think how
much more fun life would be if you used your energy to be
glad rather than worried and unhappy.

The sad thing is that *Pollyanna* has become a derogatory term
in our society. "You're such a Pollyanna" has come to mean

that you're naive and unable to see the negativity of life because you're glad to a fault. What a bunch of nonsense. We all know that life is full of challenges. It's easy to see the negative in life but it takes courage to stay positive. If you could choose between living in terror of the other shoe dropping or being in the moment and claiming the joy available to you now, which would you choose? It really is that simple.

KATHY

Life has a way of forcing you to make decisions about what you believe. I have found that life, death and miraculous events have shaped and smoothed my beliefs like constant water over stone. I consider myself to be a spiritual person. I believe my life is the perfect example that there must be a power greater than ourselves. Otherwise how did I get all the way to where I am now? People often ask me how I became a successful actor. My answer is always, "I really don't know." One minute I was a nine-year-old sitting on the front steps of my parents' house in Wisconsin, looking at my rock collection, thinking I would be an archeologist when I grew up, and the next thing I knew I was living in Hollywood and acting in a movie with Robert De Niro.

After a great deal of thought and life experience I've come to believe that this power that is greater than ourselves is in charge and I choose to call that power God. Now, it doesn't matter whether you believe in God or Buddha or Jehovah or for that matter the half-yearly white sale at Macy's. That's all up to you.

For the purpose of this story I think you need to know that I believe in a Great and Mysterious Deity that Rules the World, Knows All and Oversees Our Destiny, and I call It God.

When I was young I was entertained and comforted by my daydreaming and make-believe games. I was born with the gift of a very vivid imagination. But as I got older my imagination became something that I could use to torture myself with. If I had a headache I was afraid it was a brain tumor; if I sneezed I was certain it was pneumonia; if my elbow hurt, of course it was elbow cancer. Even if I felt happy that must mean soon all hell was about to break loose and I would lose my job, contract a horribly disfiguring disease or be kidnapped by angry rebels, who would not release me until their demands were met to have their handsome and charismatic leader set free. This last scenario was particularly imaginative as I was not employed, as you might think, at the United Nations but was working as a receptionist for a wig company.

After I moved to Los Angeles I began working with an agency as a temporary secretary and taking any job they sent me on, as I was always on the thin edge of broke. About this time I had taken up daily power walking in my neighborhood. It wasn't so much about exercising as it was about trying to outwalk the problems that were all vying for attention in my head. I wasn't making any money as an actor and it didn't look as if I would any day soon. Also, my mother's health was not good, so I was worried I was going to have to abandon all of my plans to be an actor to go back to Wisconsin and care for her. I was over-

CROWN JEWEL

> **The greater part of our happiness
> or misery depends on our dispositions,
> and not on our circumstances. We carry
> the seeds of the one or the other about
> with us in our minds wherever we go.**
> —Martha Washington

whelmed by worry and felt hopeless about being able to find solutions to my problems.

One day, as I walked down the street, there suddenly appeared in my mind's eye the image of God as CEO of a major corporation. He was sitting behind a huge old-fashioned desk and on the desk was an equally old-fashioned intercom. He said to me, "Okay, what can I do for you today?" I was very surprised and answered, "I don't know. I guess I have a lot of problems." God said, "Like what?" "Well," I said, "I'm really worried about my mother." He leaned over and, as he pressed a button on the intercom, said, "Geriatrics, what's going on with her mom?" An efficient voice very quickly answered, "We're taking care of it, God. Tell her not to worry." As he straightened up, God asked me, "What else?" I didn't have to think long before I said, "Well, I need a job." Again, he leaned over and pressed the button on the intercom. "Personnel?" "Yep, we've got something in the works. Tell her to relax—she'll have one soon." God sat up and said, "What else?"

And so it continued with all of my problems spoken and God having a department to take care of each one. When they were all dealt with, God asked, "Is there anything else?" I was at the very bottom line of my fears and said, "I'm afraid to fail, afraid to succeed, afraid to live and afraid to die." God smiled and said, "Don't worry—I'm taking care of that personally. You're safe no matter what." With all of my worries taken care of, who was I? What was my purpose? I whispered, "What am I supposed to do?" God said, "All you have to do is be happy, joyous and free—that's your job."

I felt a lightness of spirit that I hadn't felt since I was a little child. I actually began to skip down the sidewalk and stopped only because I didn't want to frighten my neighbors. I will never forget the deep sense of well-being and joy I had that morning. That profoundly healing image brought me great peace and still does.

CROWN JEWEL

The highest art is the art of living an ordinary life in an extraordinary manner.
—Tibetan Proverb

I began to grow more comfortable using imagery as a tool to heal myself. A few months later I was having one of those days filled with frustration that make you want to scream until your teeth fly out of your mouth. I started to slip into an old pattern, pulling up the long mental list of all the bad days in my life as proof that I was a total loser. This time I had the clarity to stop myself before I got too far into the long, boring list of "poor me's." It suddenly occurred to me that I had an equally long list of good things in my life but I never thought to trot those out and dwell on them. I suddenly had a memory of an add-a-pearl necklace that a little girl in my neighborhood had received as a gift. It was just a plain gold chain, and on birthdays or special occasions people would gift her pearls to add to the chain with the hopes that someday she would have a long, beautiful strand of pearls.

I decided that I would keep a mental add-a-pearl necklace. I would think of the good moments in my life as pearls and then add them to the gold chain I would keep in my mind. I began thinking of the memorable events in my life that I was grateful for and visualized each as a pearl that I placed on the chain. It was soon a long rope of gleaming pearls. Through the years I've added so many pearls that the necklace has turned into a very long coil. I imagine that each pearl has a beautiful luster from all the times I have taken the strand out and touched them to remind myself how much I have to be grateful for.

I've used imagery on many occasions to heal and comfort myself. When heading out to an audition, I visualize all the creativity of the world, past and present, floating like a shimmering violet cloud right above my head. I reach my arm straight into the air to grab hold of it. While hanging on tight, I shift ever so slightly to the right to get out of my own way and let the creativity shine through me. It's always a great reminder that the only thing that stops my creativity from flowing is me. I don't always get the job but it makes the audition so much more enjoyable.

One of my favorite imaginative moments, which I've chosen to call a spiritual experience, happened in my gray Honda Civic hatchback. It started one awful week when no matter where I went, people were paying me compliments about my work as an actor. I say *awful* because it used to be difficult for me to accept praise and, in fact, I found it quite painful. People complimented me in the grocery store, at the dry cleaner, at my temp job. I talked to a friend about it and she said, "Maybe you need to think of it as you've been given a gift. When someone offers you a compliment, thank them and then silently thank God for the gift." So that's what I did, but by the end of the week the complimenting still seemed out of control to me and I was really feeling raw and self-conscious.

After yet another person gave me a compliment while I was at the gas station, I snapped. I got in my Honda, and as I drove away I started yelling at God. "What is this about?" I shouted. "Why is everyone complimenting me? Do I have a gift and, if so, why do I have a gift? Why did Sarah Bernhardt and Mozart have a gift? I'm not saying I have that big a gift," I bellowed. "But why do *some* people have gifts and others *don't?*" Why? WHY? WHY!?! There was silence, as if I was in a vacuum, and then this thought came clearly into my head: "Don't question. Be grateful. Help others." It resonated so strongly for me that I burst into tears.

I traded that Honda in long ago but I will always be grateful for the words that came to me in it that day. They are the motto I live by. My imagination is still a great tool that I use as a balm to take the sting out of living. I've returned to God's office many times to lay out my fears and have him delegate them to the necessary department so I can get back to my job of being happy, joyous and free.

I often feel as if I am just one click away from bliss. It seems like all the vibrant light of the universe is trying to enter my body so it can fill me and then burst back out of my toes, fingers, eyes, knees and even my eyelashes. The only thing that stops me from being this brilliant and joyful in my life is me. Old thoughts of low self-esteem and fear hold me back. Decisions made long ago that helped me then, but are no longer valid, stop me from lighting up like a giant pinwheel and showering sparks of joy into my life and onto the lives of those around me.

I've worked very hard to let go of the things that pull me out of the happiness of the moment. I make the conscious choice each day to be grateful. I'm not a silly, naive optimist. I've been around the block more than a few times, so I know bad things happen. They've happened to me. Yet, I make the choice daily to stay out of worry and live my life finding great joy in the moment. I'm glad I'm not afraid to be called a Pollyanna.

• • •

Of course, you can't be happy every moment of life. And don't worry, we're not talking about the kind of euphoric happiness where your face hurts from constantly smiling and people are a bit frightened of you. We're talking about taking the fleeting feeling of "life is good" and, with practice, turning it into the comfortable, steady hum of happiness that becomes the undercurrent of a good life.

You definitely have the skill to discover how to live in the positive. With no formal training and very little thought you've taught yourself to actively be negative. If you make the decision to be happy you will improve the quality of the rest of your life. Spending your precious time in the positive, attracting even more positive, is a great gift to give yourself.

Maybe it helps to look at the idea this way. Negative thought and positive thought attract like-minded thinking into your life. Which one do you want? Because the choice is really yours.

CINDY

About thirty years ago, on a lark, I visited a gypsy tearoom in New York City. It was on the second floor of a building on Lexington Avenue, right across from Bloomingdale's. You paid ten dollars at the door and got a cupful of lukewarm water with lots of loose tea leaves floating in it. You had to swill the "tea," sit down in their waiting room and wait for the next available gypsy.

When my turn finally came, the gypsy took my cup, looked inside and said, "You should get a makeover. You need to wear more makeup. Go over to Bloomingdale's. They always have someone doing makeovers at the makeup counters."

This was not exactly the life-affirming, visionary advice I was searching for, and since I'd already paid my ten bucks, I thought I might as well ask a question, so I threw out, "Will I be successful?" She looked at the tea leaves but they were apparently just advising a makeover, so she whipped out her tarot cards and began laying them down. "You will always have enough but you'll have to work very hard for it. It will never come easily to you." She then grabbed the cup, thrust it toward my face so I could see that the tea leaves weren't lying and again advised me to rush over to Bloomingdale's for a makeover.

CROWN JEWEL

Life is the only real counselor; wisdom unfiltered through personal experience does not become a part of the moral tissue.

—Edith Wharton

I ignored her advice about going to Bloomingdale's but for some reason I have never been able to shake the sound of her voice telling me that, although I would have enough, I would always have to work very hard for it.

At times I've been comforted by the gypsy's prediction that I'll always have enough. But at other times, when I wanted to just stay home and enjoy my life and my family, I would feel great frustration because I would hear the gypsy saying, "You'll have to work very hard for it…" So instead of enjoying the life I was creating, I would work evenings and weekends because I thought "it will never come easily to you" was my destiny.

When I was first laid off and trying to start my own business, it was very stressful. Not only was I hearing the gypsy's voice, but I was also battling the entire Mongol Horde. There were days when I got very little accomplished because my focus was devoured by worry—worry that the hard times would last longer than the cushion we had managed to save, worry that when the money ran out, I wouldn't be able to pay the mortgage or be able to afford my unbelievably expensive health insurance or even be able to put food on the table.

Out of fear I would scan the newspapers for jobs—any jobs. I practiced saying, "Welcome to Walmart" and "Would you like to supersize that?" My fear made my thinking very black-and-white and I would jump right to thoughts like, "I can sell my house and we can live in a trailer park and I can take in laundry." I would completely miss the possibility that there might be other solutions somewhere between tightening our belts and reliving *The Grapes of Wrath*.

Some days when my fear and anxiety about the future were extra strong, the Mongol Horde would show up with their pet—a huge fire-breathing dragon. The great scaly beast, with fire and smoke curling from its nostrils, would circle my home, pounding on doors and rattling the glass as it glared at me through the windows. It felt as if at any moment it would crash through the walls and engulf me in flames.

It takes a lot of energy to fight a dragon, almost as much as it takes to create one. My fear was pulling me out of the moment and placing me in a very anxious and danger-filled future. It sapped the joy out of my day and left me drained, emotionally and physically.

I've had my share of grief and sadness in my life but the truth is that a lot of my unhappiness has been created by me. I was so busy borrowing worry from the future, about things that were probably never going to happen, that I was destroying any chance of happiness in my present. I had no gratitude for all the abundance I did have and no faith that I would be able to hang on to any of it. I didn't understand that being happy and worry free is a choice, and making that choice on a daily basis takes practice.

CROWN JEWEL

The art of being happy lies in the power of extracting happiness from common things.
—Henry Ward Beecher

To help keep the dragon, the Mongol Horde and the gypsy at bay I've learned to use the tool of gratitude. On a cold night, when the warmth of my fireplace comforts me, instead of worrying about if I'll be able to afford wood next winter, I choose to be grateful for the fire that warms me now. When a silly game of cards around the kitchen table causes peals of laughter from the youngest member of our household, instead of worrying about what the future holds for him, I make the choice to be grateful that we are together right now and smiling. When watching my husband chop vegetables for one of his famous homemade soups, I no longer worry if we will always be able to afford the ingredients, and make the choice to be grateful that I have a wonderful husband who makes a great bowl of soup.

Something a ten-dollar gypsy said to me thirty years ago made me believe that abundance was not in the cards for me unless I worked for it, like I was on a chain gang. As if I were living in a novel by one of the Brontë sisters, I believed that I had to suffer in order to be worthy of anything I received. I thought if something came too easily to me, I hadn't earned it and therefore didn't deserve to enjoy it. I now believe that life is supposed to be easy and joyful. When it is difficult and painful, it's a sign that I need to change something.

I'm the protector of my realm. I choose to armor myself with optimism and the faith that everything will be all right no matter what, because my life experience has shown me that. I practice finding joy in the everyday details of my life and believing I am worthy of abundance.

• • •

We told you we would give you a simple trick to help you be happy. Here it is...drumroll, please—*you just have to decide to be happy.* Honest, it really is that simple. But simple doesn't necessarily mean easy. It takes a bit of practice, but trust us, it's oh so worth it.

You make decisions every day that you hope will protect you and provide you with what you need to live and keep you safe. Is it such a leap of faith to believe that you can also make the decision to be happy? If you can learn to grumble about the negative things in life, you can certainly become skilled at seeing the positive things so that you can be grateful and happy.

WHAT WE DID AND STILL DO TO CHOOSE HAPPINESS

We use imagery and gratitude and practice daily. For us, making the decision to be happy also means making our lives a fun place to be. We truly give ourselves lots of extra points for making ourselves laugh.

Kathy uses imagery almost on a daily basis to deal with everything from stress to anger. Last week she found herself filled with road rage after an irresponsible driver almost ran her off the road. Instead of staying angry, she visualized placing the driver into a giant jar filled with jewelry cleaner and swirling him around in it till he was a better driver. She made herself laugh and her anger began to slip away.

When we were sending out proposals to interest publishers in this book, one of the things we included was our bios. Months later, after all the packets had gone out and we had sold the book, one of Cindy's friends asked for written material about us that she could give to someone who was thinking of hiring us as speakers for an event. We updated the packets, including our bios, and sent them to her. Her friend e-mailed Cindy within hours to let her know there was a spelling error in her bio. Instead of reading that Cindy had begun her career as a *public*-relations specialist, it read *pubic*-relations specialist. We laughed until we cried. On Cindy's gratitude list that night was the word *ten*. She was grateful we had sent out only ten proposals instead of a hundred.

After an initial period of working daily on our gratitude, we are now on the "gratitude maintenance program." Moments of gratitude now present themselves without great effort on our part. Sometimes they are small, as in being grateful on a hot summer day that someone invented air-conditioning. On other days we are overwhelmed with gratitude for the love of family and friends. By letting go of our "I'll be happy when's," and making the simple decision to be happy, we have now created lives that we are truly grateful for.

HERE'S WHAT YOU CAN DO

If you're worried that you don't have a vivid imagination like Kathy, don't be. Here's an easy way to begin the practice of choosing to be happy. Pick one thing every morning to be glad about and one more thing every night before you go to sleep. Do this to get in the practice of noticing the things that are already good in your life. In the beginning keep it simple. In the morning you might say, "I'm glad I woke up" or "I'm glad somebody discovered coffee." At night it could be something like, "I'm glad I own a pillow" or "I'm glad I have some teeth to brush." You get extra points if you make yourself laugh.

Keep a notepad by your bed and jot down the things you're glad about as you think of them. We know you're busy, so keep the writing simple. There may be days when you think there is nothing to be glad about at all. On those days take a look at the list you've been keeping. We feel confident you'll see something there that will help jog your memory and bring out your inner Pollyanna.

As you daily add more things to the glad list, it will become easier and more natural to feel happy. After the initial fun of being glad for teeth, bed linens and coffee, you will uncover a deeper list of glads. You will find that, much sooner than you think, you will be able to focus on what's good in your life right now and easily let go of the thought patterns that stand in the way of your happiness. With continued practice we promise you'll discover this simple trick really works. So, be a proud Pollyanna and join us in giving yourself the gift of choosing happiness.

ROYAL PROCLAMATION

I, the Queen, will fire up my imagination so that
each day I can find something to be glad about.
I will embrace my inner Pollyanna, without fear
or embarrassment, and make the choice to be
happy. I will create my own add-a-pearl necklace
of gratitude and wear it with royal pride.

CHAPTER 8

celebrate [se-lə-brāt] (verb) 1. mark an occasion 2. show happiness at something 3. rejoice 4. commemorate 5. have fun 6. enjoy yourself 7. make merry 8. party

PROCLAIM YOURSELF QUEEN OF YOUR OWN LIFE

...or...

The Crowning Ceremony

Congratulations! You've mastered talking to the mirror, stood on the Windy Mountain and got your hair all messed up, battled the Mongol Horde, gathered trusted LIW, repelled the Huns and made the decision to be happy. Hip hip hooray! It's time to put on the crown and be the Queen. So, start thinking about the kind of party you want to throw yourself, because that's what this chapter is all about.

As we told you in our introduction, we feel strongly that there is a need for a celebration to mark a woman's transition into the second half of her life. That's why we created the Crowning Ceremony to celebrate this most significant moment in our lives. So, with finger foods, perhaps a lovely beverage or two and trusted friends, we say, "Let the coronation begin."

CROWN JEWEL

**Age is something that doesn't matter,
unless you are a cheese.**

—Billie Burke

In Chapter 1 we told you about our Crowning Ceremony, which took place in Prague and lasted a full week. Since then we've been involved in many crownings. Some have been intimate, with just one or two friends over scrambled eggs and coffee, while others have been large, lively evenings filled with strangers and massive amounts of food, all shaped like crowns. None of them have lasted for longer than a few hours but they've all been equally powerful, life affirming and just plain fun.

We're going to give you some general guidelines on how we host a Crowning Ceremony, but only if you promise not to follow them to the letter of the law. The most important thing is to create the kind of party you want to go to. This ceremony is celebrating your transition, so it needs to reflect your likes and desires. Do you enjoy pomp and circumstance or colored lights and feathered boas, or are you a beer-and-bratwurst woman? You figure it out and plan accordingly. You're the only one you have to please. So, with our warning firmly in place, let's get started.

WHAT WE DID TO PROCLAIM OURSELVES QUEENS OF OUR OWN LIVES

We both love to entertain and for us a good party starts with the invitation. Sending out glorious formal invitations printed on creamy paper with a big embossed Q would be perfect. Unfortunately we don't have the time to shop for, address and mail that kind of invitation, so we just send out clever e-mails. It works for us.

There are lots of props involved in our Crowning Ceremony so, for us, this is a great excuse to indulge our love of being creative on our computers. With very little effort we've designed a Crowning Ceremony Card to be given to all the guests. Our card has Queen of Your Own Life on the front, and inside we have printed two columns, headed Banish and Keep, as well as a fill-in-the-blank Royal Proclamation to be read by each new Queen at the end of the ceremony.

It occurred to us that it would be nice to be able to give our guests an official commemorative crowning certificate to take home. At the office-supply store we found packages of blank certificates in great colors that were perfect. We created a template with some queenly clip art and official "You Are Crowned" language and printed it on the blank certificates. Sometimes, if there are only a few guests, we get carried away and hand-tint the certificates. Other times, if it's going to be a big crowd, the certificates look just fine to us the way they are. We are big advocates of fun and stress-free gatherings.

QUEEN
OF YOUR OWN
LIFE

BANISH   KEEP

....
....
....
....
....

IT'S OFFICIAL—YOU'RE CROWNED

Statement of power: I................................am Queen of My Own Life.
I will use my power to decide each day to live my life
without judgment and to enjoy myself fully.

As my first official act, I choose to

....
....
....
....

OUR CROWNING KIT

Sign-in Sheet	Crown
Lovely Pens	Certificates
Note Cards	Fireworks (optional)
Talking Scepter	Candles
Crown Brooch (attractive)	Beverages
	Cake

On the night of the big event, as the women arrive, we ask them to put their names and e-mail addresses or phone numbers on a sign-in sheet so that we can stay in touch after the ceremony (it's fun when a recently crowned Queen reports back on some new regal behavior). We then give them the cards we've created and, in addition, gift each woman an attractive pen for note taking. Then we point them toward the food and beverages and say, "Enjoy."

After everyone has arrived and some festive mingling and snacking have occurred, we invite everyone to sit down. To begin the ceremony, we welcome everybody and begin using another of our props. We have a shiny, bejeweled but inexpensive scepter that we call the "talking scepter." Whoever is holding it has the floor and may speak. We bought ours online but you can get them at a party store, or if you're crafty you can make your own. Again, because it is your party, you may decide to skip the talking scepter altogether and just point.

As the hostesses we immediately let the guests know we are not there to sell them jewelry or to involve them in a pyramid scheme; we've brought them together for a ceremony to celebrate with us the transition from the first half of our lives to what will surely be the best half of our lives.

We ask them to take a look at the cards we've given them and to think about these two questions:

* What do you want to let go of or banish from the first half of your life that no longer works for you or makes you happy?
* What do you want to keep from the first half of your life that makes you strong and gives you joy?

We encourage the guests to use the attractive pen we've given them to jot down their thoughts and feelings about these questions in the appropriate columns on the card, as well as any responses to the proclamation. We let them know that after we tell our stories we'll be giving them an opportunity to share what they've written.

At this point we talk about our own choices in the Banish and Keep columns. We make it short but honest. For example, Cindy might say, "When I lost my job, I felt ashamed, because it made me feel like I had failed, when the truth was, the company was downsizing and it wasn't personal. I want to banish beating myself up about things that I have no control over. What I want to keep is the sense of adventure and excitement I had in my twenties that allowed me to move to New York with only two hundred dollars in my pocket and start a whole new life." Kathy might say, "I come from a place of below-sea-level self-esteem and always found it hard to believe that I deserved good things. I want to banish my belief that I'm not good enough. I want to keep my ability to find humor every day, which helps make my life enjoyable."

We have found that our level of honesty and openness sets the mood and the tone for the gathering. By creating a safe atmosphere we want to be able to give each woman permission to focus her energy and attention on herself without fear of judgment from anybody—including herself.

When women talk to one another about their own journeys and disclose their issues with self-esteem and claiming their power, the common ground we share is revealed. Realizing that we are all so much alike is the base for creating a much-needed community of support. The knowledge that we are not alone in our struggles becomes the basis for healing and gathering the strength needed to claim the power to become the best Queen of Your Own Life…. And we get to do it all while eating cake!

When we finish speaking we randomly pass the talking scepter around the room, inviting each woman to share what she has written in the columns on her card. Many universal issues come up time and again in the Banish column: low

CROWN JEWEL

**You gain strength, courage and
confidence by every experience in which
you really stop to look fear in the face.
You are able to say to yourself, "I lived
through this horror. I can take the next thing
that comes along." You must do the things
you think you cannot do.**

—Eleanor Roosevelt

self-esteem, fear of not being liked or being thought unlovable, putting others ahead of your own needs and fear of taking risks, to name only a few.

It turns out the Keep column is often more challenging because we are so uncomfortable identifying, naming and just plain saying, out loud, what our strengths are. The good news is that in revealing to ourselves and others that we have such positive qualities as courage, perseverance or a well-developed sense of humor, we are given the chance to acknowledge and accept how amazing we really are.

Finally, after everyone has answered the two questions, it's time for the official crowning. We have an old jeweled crown that we bought at a garage sale that we bring out at this point. We then randomly choose a woman and hand her the crown and scepter, giving her the option to wear the crown or not (not a single woman has ever chosen not to wear it; in fact, most of the time we have to nudge them to take the crown off).

We ask the woman to read the personal proclamation she has written on her card. We already have most of it written out for her, so, for example, it might look like this: *I, (your name), am now Queen of My Own Life. I will use my power to decide each day to live my life without judgment and to enjoy myself fully. As my first official act, I choose to (fill in the blank).*

When she is done reading her proclamation, we pin her with an attractive crown-shaped brooch and give her the certificate stating that she is now the Queen. There is usually some queenly waving, lots of clapping and, if she is agreeable, some photo taking with the crown on. Then the new Queen chooses the next woman and passes on the scepter and crown.

This step is repeated until every woman has read her proclamation. We retrieve the talking scepter and crown and officially declare everyone to be Queen of Your Own Life. Imagine at this point loud applause erupting with everyone saying, "Hear! Hear!" and "Hail the Queens!" Lots of hugging and toasting ensue and we all head back to the buffet for more beverages and cake.

We are often made humble by the new Queen's willingness to be candid and honest as she proclaims her first official act. If we've done our job as hostesses and made the room a safe place, we sometimes hear a proclamation that is deeply heartfelt. As when Queen V. declared, "From this day forward I want to be known as Queen V. the Funny and not Queen V. the Sick."

CROWN JEWEL

**Dance as though no one is watching,
love as though you have never been hurt,
sing as though no one can hear you,
and live as though heaven is on earth.**

—Father Alfred D'Souza

There was an outpouring of support for her with everyone agreeing unanimously, "That is who she will be to us from this moment on!" At another crowning everyone cheered as Queen L. vowed to stop climbing the corporate ladder and added that, by this time next year, she would be a volunteer with the Peace Corps.

More often than not a new Queen's first official act is something so funny we all find ourselves laughing out loud. Like when Queen C. stated that from this day forward she would have more sex with her husband. Oh, the heads nodded in agreement at that one. At one crowning a new Queen announced, to much cheering, that she would eat chocolate for breakfast and not feel guilty. At yet another ceremony one of the Queens, whose husband loved to camp, promised she would overcome her aversion to outdoor etiquette and finally learn to go to the bathroom in the woods. A proclamation we hear often from a lot of new Queens is, "I will be a good friend to myself first so I can be a good friend to others." Whether the first official act is serious or lighthearted, they are all met with agreement and universal support.

HERE'S WHAT YOU CAN DO

Now it's your turn. Our Crowning Ceremony is simple, but as we've mentioned, yours can be anything you want it to. Some women have said they gathered lots of friends, lit candles and burned their Banish list, while others simply met with one or two friends and held their ceremony over lunch. We encourage everyone to add their own flair and drama to the ritual to make it as magical and powerful as they like. Feel free to repeat the ceremony as often as necessary to reinforce your newfound royal status as Queen of Your Own Life.

·········· CROWN JEWEL ··········

Striving for excellence motivates you; striving for perfection is demoralizing.
—Harriet Braiker

The only way to mess this up is to not give yourself the gift of a Crowning Ceremony. It's important that you celebrate this moment so that you and everyone around you can formally honor your unique journey and what a fabulous woman you've become. Again, don't worry about trying to throw the perfect party. If your first Crowning is just you, this book and a cupcake, that's fine. As we said, you can have as many Crowning Ceremonies as you like—in as many ways as you like.

Here are a couple of ideas. You can combine your crowning with any number of other kinds of gatherings. Invite your friends to read a great book that honors and empowers women and then have them come over for a Book Club Crowning Ceremony. You could even do it every month. It's a great excuse to celebrate yourself and your friends. If you and your LIW are crafty, you could combine a Crowning Ceremony with a crown-making party so that each new Queen gets her own royal accessory to take home. We heartily support your right to use hot-melt glue guns and glitter pens.

Another great idea is to have your ceremony during a "girl-friend getaway." Check schedules with your LIW and plan it for a destination you have always wanted to go to, like a little inn near the ocean, a bed-and-breakfast in the Rockies, a spa in the desert or even Paris. The point is to just do it. You've worked so hard and come so far and you're more than ready. If not now, when?

To help spark your creativity we have lots of downloadable templates, like the Crowning Ceremony Card and the You Are Crowned Certificate, on our Web site at http://www.queenofyourownlife.com. Another fun template you'll find at our site is a blank coat of arms for you to print and decorate. When we created ours, we used the virtues we had chosen for our Queen and added color, our photos and a motto. As always, you are limited only by your imagination. It can be as elaborate or as simple as you choose. A blank coat of arms and a package of colored pens or crayons make a fun gift for the newly crowned Queens to take home and decorate at their leisure. In the end it's the simple gifts that are the most fun.

············ CROWN JEWEL ···············

**You are unique and if that is not fulfilled,
then something has been lost.**
—Martha Graham

PERSONAL COAT OF ARMS

That's it. You now know everything you need to in order to throw yourself one terrific Crowning Ceremony. An added bonus is that it's a party that truly keeps on giving. By staying in touch with the newly crowned Queens, we have found that we've been inspired by what they tell us about their new status as Queens of Our Own Lives. There is strength in being part of this community of strong women, so we encourage you to take the time to stay in touch. Here are some of the wonderful things women have shared with us.

★

"Watching the hugs, tears and encouragement from everyone was absolutely amazing. I felt empowered and wonderful, so much so that I was able to get through the following evening with my in-laws with minimal stress and aggravation. Seriously, when I shared the events of the crowning with my sisters-in-law (aged sixty-plus), it began a dialogue that mimicked the feelings brought out at the party. They, too, identified and loved the concept." —**Queen D.**

★

"It was fabulous. And it is good to be Queen!" —**Queen C.**

★

"I keep my crown pin in my bedside table drawer, and whenever I need extra strength, I take it out and wear it proudly!" —**Queen C.**

★

"I was inspired to reimagine the book I've been working on, outline it in its entirety and complete a sample section. I am sending it off to a new agent and I'm very energized and excited about the possibilities." —**Queen R.**

★

"I've been meaning to thank you for the very special evening.... I have to say, I was amazed at the openness of the group. It was apparent that every woman has things on her mind that no one would ever guess— and that a simple invitation to share can be so enlightening and empowering." —**Queen V.**

★

"Being crowned Queen of My Own Life made me feel blessed. I have a wonderful family, fulfilling job, good health and really nothing I have any right to complain about. True, I'm tired, way too busy and usually rushed, but the Crowning Ceremony reminded me that everyone else is, too! Each morning my crown twinkles up at me from its special spot in my jewelry box and reminds me that all will be well and that I really don't look all that fat in the outfit I'm wearing. I remember my fellow Queens in a quick prayer and focus on the positive." —**Queen D.**

★

"When I woke up the day after my crowning, I cried. Who knew that all the people I thought were so strong and had it all 'together' were just like me, trying to keep it together. Since that day I now don't feel like I am the only one who has crap in their life that they need to let go of. I have let go of a lot and am working on the rest. Who knows…maybe I can be the woman I know I am capable of being. I am Queen of My Own Life—I now say it and almost always believe it." **—Queen P.**

★

"I just wanted to make sure I properly thanked you for the Crowning Ceremony. You were right—it was empowering and fun at the same time, with quite a range of emotions, from crying to laughing. The two women I asked to come with me from work enjoyed the whole night… We all wore and showed off our pins at work. You both are inspiring to all women and I hope I can be like you and not worry about what people think of me. I will have to work on that." **—Queen K.**

★

"I've framed my crowning certificate and hung it near my bed so that I can see it when I wake up. Each day as I look at it, I think to myself, If not now, when? *I am truly more than ready to be Queen of My Own Life."* **—Queen S.**

You are poised on the edge of the second half of your life. You can choose to make it the best half. Give yourself this final gift—proclaim yourself Queen of Your Own Life and do it with one heck of a spectacular party. You deserve it!

ROYAL PROCLAMATION

From this day forward, I will remember I am
an extraordinary woman—beautiful, intelligent,
brave and powerful. With the wisdom and tools
that I have gained, I am excited to embark on the
adventure that is the glorious second half
of my life. I am now truly the
Queen of My Own Life.

EPILOGUE

fabulous [fa-byə-ləs] (adjective) 1. incredible
2. marvelous 3. wonderful 4. tremendous
5. amazing 6. remarkable 7. great 8. extraordinary

EPILOGUE

....

OKAY, I'M QUEEN OF MY OWN LIFE

...or...

Now What Can I Do?

You did it. You are the Queen of Your Own Life. You've given yourself the gifts and gathered all the necessary tools to live a spectacular second half of your life. Keep in mind the more you use the tools, the easier it will get to be the best possible Queen you can be.

Writing this book was transformational for us. Life continued to happen while we worked on this project and we relied heavily on each other and our friendship to get us through both the living and the writing. We did it by holding up the mirror for one another so that we were able to see our best selves reflected there. We had already claimed the seven gifts that we offered to you in Chapter 1. Yet we're not exaggerating when we say that working to share the Queen philosophy with you truly cemented the seven gifts firmly in our lives.

We have a secret to tell you. You already were the Queen of Your Own Life. You just needed a couple of good friends like us to hold up the mirror to help you see what we see—your best self, a woman who has been made wiser and stronger by the journey, who is beautiful just the way she is and who is more than capable of creating a life for herself that is filled with joy.

The key to keeping your newfound royal status is to pass it on. Help other women claim their power, beauty and happiness by talking about how you discovered yours. Have another crowning party and invite at least one woman you don't know very well. Share how you felt when you were crowned and what positive changes you've had in your life since then. Drink lovely beverages. Eat more cake.

We believe that the more honest, brave, generous and loving you are (or whatever queenly virtues you've chosen), the more you will attract like-minded people into your life. In the end the practice of living your life in a royal way will enrich not only your life but the lives of everyone around you.

Now, go be fabulous. You really *are* Queen of Your Own Life, not just because we say so, but because you say so.

In royal fondness,

Queen Cindy and *Queen Kathy*

QUEEN
OF YOUR OWN
LIFE

NAME

YOU'RE MORE THAN READY

SO, IF NOT NOW, WHEN?

The extraordinary woman named above has completed
her crowning ceremony on the ____ day of ____, 20 ____,
and is now Queen of Her Own Life.

AS WITNESSED BY:

Queen Kathy Kinney   Queen Cindy Ratzlaff

NOTE TO SELF

1. *Have more fun.*
2.

NOTE TO SELF

_____

_____

_____

_____

_____

_____

_____

_____

_____

_____

_____

_____

_____

_____

_____

NOTE TO SELF

NOTE TO SELF

NOTE TO SELF

ABOUT THE AUTHORS

Kathy Kinney is best known for her iconic role as Mimi Bobeck on *The Drew Carey Show*. She has acted in more than a dozen films and guest starred on numerous television shows. Kathy, whose background is in improvisational comedy, toured with Drew Carey and the Improv All-Stars for the USO in Iraq and Saudi Arabia and may still be seen performing with Drew and the All-Stars in Las Vegas. Currently coproducing a project for children on the Internet aimed at furthering literacy and keeping alive the joy of books and reading, Kathy may also be seen at http://www.mrsp.com in the title role of Mrs. P.

Cindy Ratzlaff was named to the prestigious *Advertising Age*'s Marketing 50 list for the blockbuster launch of *The South Beach Diet* in the same year that Steve Jobs made the list for the launch of the iPod. A veteran publishing executive, Cindy created marketing and publicity campaigns for more than one hundred *New York Times* bestselling books, including Dr. Perricone's *The Wrinkle Cure,* Jorge Cruise's *8 Minutes in the Morning* and Dr. Shapiro's *Picture Perfect Weight Loss.* As president of her own marketing and brand strategy firm, Brand New Brand You, she specializes in using new social media platforms to increase brand awareness.